Create a Signature You Love

A step-by-step guide to designing and perfecting the best signature for you

Written by Brooke Vega

All illustrations by Adina Cioran [Cadina]
Book design by Miriam Castro

Printed in the United States of America
First Printing, 2018

ISBN 978-1-7337836-0-6

Visit https://createasignature.com
support@createasignature.com

Table of Contents

Preface

"Art-Shame" and Learning to Learn

66 *A few modern philosophers...assert that an individual's intelligence is a fixed quantity, a quantity which cannot be increased. We must protest and react against this brutal pessimism.... With practice, training, and above all, method, we manage to increase our attention, our memory, our judgment, and literally to become more intelligent than we were before.* 99

— Alfred Binet, *Inventor of the IQ Test*

66 *People can't do something themselves, they wanna tell you you can't do it. You want something, go get it. Period.* 99

— Christopher Gardner, *The Pursuit of Happyness*

I often reflect upon the good old days, when my artistic ability was on par with that of my peers – when I could draw expressively and unselfconsciously, taking risks with color and composition, and no subject matter was "too ambitious" for my skill level. Unfortunately, that hasn't been the case since kindergarten.

Sometime around first or second grade, things started to change. I remember completing a drawing during art class, holding my work up in front of my face to admire it, my consciousness slowly returning from the place of focus and joy that it had inhabited while I was creating.

I felt good.

Then, looking to my right to see what my best friend had drawn, I experienced a moment of pure shock and fear. At the time, I had no knowledge of perspective, lines, values, or any of the other tools artists use to produce aesthetically pleasing work – but in that moment, I knew one thing with a certainty simpler than breathing: hers was *good*, and mine was *bad*. All I could think was, "What happened? How did she do that? What did I miss?"

Shortly thereafter, I compared some handwritten work with that of another friend, and experienced a similar cocktail of emotions which foreshadowed the handwriting, signature, and general art-shame I would often feel in the years to come. Her writing was tidy, smooth, consistent; she used the space on the page intelligently. Mine, in plain contrast, was almost comically large, awkwardly spaced, and disorganized. I had no concept of how much space on the page a sentence would occupy until after I finished writing it, I gripped my writing utensils as though they might unexpectedly break free and attack me, and I pressed down so hard on the paper I could probably have carved letters into stone without additional effort. But I didn't perceive any of these nuances. I sat there, thinking in the simple terms of "good" and "bad," utterly dumbfounded as to how this had happened.

It was so jarring. I truly loved to learn, I was never afraid to work hard, and there were many other areas in which I seemed to excel. My verbal and writing abilities, for example, were often the focus of the praise I received from family and teachers. My parents told, and retold, stories about how many words I could say at nine months old, and how I could speak in full sentences at one year. They commented "it was almost scary," and that my small size coupled with my large vocabulary "freaked some people out." They reminded me that, at three or four years old, after being given a book by my grandmother, I had sanguinely, yet matter-of-factly set about the task of teaching myself to read. Naïve and full of hope about my future, I often felt a swell of pride upon hearing these stories. They made me believe I was special and gifted, and I filed them away carefully, as testaments to my intelligence and innate talents.

And yet, the artistic competence of my friends seemed to have developed naturally, while mine had remained stagnant. How did artistic skill pass me by without me even noticing? I didn't know the answer with the clarity of words – but I felt it. I felt a deficiency, a failure, inside of me. If my verbal ability, which often felt effortless, made me seem "gifted" in the eyes of others, what did these artistic failures make me?

World-renowned psychologist Carol Dweck has spent years studying how children cope with failure. This research led her to make a groundbreaking contribution to her field when she described the two broad belief systems that people have about intelligence and ability. She calls these belief systems the "fixed mindset" and the "growth mindset."

A person with a fixed mindset views learning (either in general or in relation to specific tasks) as being tied to innate and immutable ability. Results in learning are seen as a function of raw talent; i.e. a fixed mindset child with a poor grade in math class might say "I'm not good at math" or even, tragically, "I'm not smart enough." If the same child experiences success in writing or sports, he might say "I'm really creative" or "I've always been athletic." Whether the child is experiencing success or failure, ability is described as a feature of who the child is, and the outcome is explained as an inevitable expression of that feature. The emphasis in this mindset is on *fixed, inborn human characteristics or capacities*.

By contrast, a person with a growth mindset essentially believes that intelligence and talent can be developed. Learning, therefore, is understood as a long-term process where results are primarily a function of effort expended, time spent, quality of instruction or materials, etc. A child with a growth mindset, experiencing the same setbacks and achievements from the examples above, might respond to them by saying "I need to study harder for math class," and "I'm getting good at writing/sports because I have a great teacher/coach and I practice all the time." The emphasis is on *behaviors*.

Dweck has found that these mindsets are instrumental factors in whether people succeed in reaching their potential, and in whether they have a positive relationship to learning. While the growth mindset has been linked to enjoyment of learning, resilience in the face of setbacks, and mastery, the fixed mindset has been linked to decreased self-confidence, brittle resolve, and learned helplessness.

Why?

In the face of failure, people with the fixed mindset tend to feel not only that they *have failed in this instance*, but that they *are failures*. Even in success, "fixed mindsetters" link their self-worth to their results. As Dweck puts it in her important book, *Mindset: The New Psychology of Success*, "Believing that your qualities are carved in stone... creates an urgency to prove yourself over and over. If you only have a certain amount of intelligence, a certain personality, and a certain moral character, well, then you'd better prove that you have a healthy dose of them. It simply wouldn't do to look or feel deficient in these most basic characteristics." But since all real learning and growth inevitably require mistakes, losses, and failures along the way, people with the fixed mindset often end up trapped inside small comfort zones, racked with anxiety and doubt, afraid that a mistake will dispel their "talented" or "smart" image. Ultimately, they are often unable to stay the course to mastery.

But, back in my elementary school classes, impressed by the work of my friends and bewildered by its contrast with mine, I didn't know any of that.

My curiosity, enthusiasm, and considerable grit notwithstanding, I concluded, "I am not an artistic person." This made sense to me. It fit. Some people were born with this gift, and some weren't. That neatly explained why the artwork and handwriting of some kids continued to improve, while that of others (like myself) did not. I had other strengths, but I wasn't built to produce beautiful pictures or letters. I leaned into a fixed mindset, effectively banning myself from an entire area of interest because of my perceived deficiency and hanging more importance than ever on my "natural gifts," with which I sought to compensate.

From then on, I marveled at artists as though they were magicians with access to some secret power that was off limits to me, I drooled over the confident, fluid strokes of my friends' signatures and envied the elusive inner spirit that I thought made them possible. I secretly wished, truly, deeply, and often, that I could have that talent. But it could not be learned. You were born either right-brained or left-brained, visual or logical, creative or analytical – but, except in exceedingly rare cases, you could not be both.

It was a long time before I stopped believing this.

The truth is, my literary success can be explained primarily by the fact that I spent enormous chunks of my free time reading and writing – in other words, analyzing examples of quality writing and practicing. By contrast, I rarely spent time drawing, had few examples of the process of creating visual art, and effectively quit trying to improve my handwriting and signature pretty early on.

It is, perhaps, unsurprising that I all but lost my motivation to improve my signature after I had concluded that I wasn't the kind of person who could have good handwriting. Still, I briefly felt the desire to shrink away and hide, as well as the trademark hot flash followed by cold sweat that accompanies all my episodes of shame, each time I signed my name on an important document - my passport, my driver's license, my first (and second, and third...) job offer acceptance letter.

In the grand scheme of life, it may seem a small thing, but each time I signed my name, it felt like I was revealing my incredible lack of artistic endowment. I simply couldn't reconcile with the fact that I could possibly perform so poorly at something I had been doing for so many years. It felt like something I **should** be able to do. Letting another person see my messy signature, which hadn't improved an ounce since childhood, felt like admitting to them that I couldn't spell my own name.

Thankfully, that wasn't all I felt. Some stubborn, yet optimistic, part of me refused to fully accept that there was something I was incapable of doing as well as I wanted to. Deep down, I sensed that this idea that our capacities are predetermined and finite did not represent the true face of the world.

In the last several years, this possibility has become a fascination and a passion to me. I've invested countless hours researching and experimenting with learning how to learn better. What I've found, both in theory and in practice, is that the gifts we are born with – or without – need have little bearing on our futures. You can develop your intelligence, your creativity, and your mindset.

Consider the following study, cited by Dweck in *Mindset*, "Benjamin Bloom, an eminent educational researcher, studied 120 outstanding achievers. They were concert pianists, sculptors, Olympic swimmers, world-class tennis players, and mathematicians. Most were not that remarkable as children and didn't show clear talent before their training began in earnest.... Bloom concludes, 'After forty years of intensive research on school learning in the United States as well as abroad, my major conclusion is: What any person in the world can learn, *almost* all persons can learn, if provided with the appropriate prior and current conditions of learning.' He's not counting the two to three percent of children who have severe learning impairments, and he's not counting the top one to two percent of children at the other extreme.... He *is* counting everybody else."

Most skills are acquired when a person focuses on and practices with the right materials, consistently, over time. Math is a skill. Art is a skill. Signatures are a skill. In this book, I will show you which materials to focus on, teach you how to stay consistent, and help you create a signature you love in the shortest time possible.

If I can do it, you can do it .

—
Original Signature

—
New Signature

Introduction

❝ *Art when really understood is the province of every human being. It is simply a question of doing things, anything, well. It is not an outside, extra thing.* ❞

                                                    — Robert Henri, *The Art Spirit*

What makes a signature "good?"

The answer to this question varies somewhat depending upon whom you ask, but we all instinctively recognize a gorgeous signature when we see one. Those jaw-dropping, awe-inspiring works of art, executed in no time, which seem to leave no doubt as to the competence and personality of the signer.

This type of signature is the goal, but in order to create one for ourselves, we have to get a bit more specific about which qualities make us swoon.

Let's do a quick review of some important terms to make that conversation easier. You may wish to bookmark this page for ease of reference later on. We'll continue using all of these terms throughout the book, and they are important to understand.

Signature

ascender line

x-height
baseline

descender line

Baseline:	The line (whether real or imagined) the letters "sit" on top of.
X-height:	The distance from the baseline to the top of lowercase letters, not counting ascenders.
Ascender:	The portion of extended lowercase letters which rises above the x-height.
Descender:	The portion of extended lowercase letters which drops below the baseline.
Slant:	The angle at which the letters lean. It can be leftward, upright, or rightward.

Almost any visually appealing signature will have the following characteristics:

1. Legibility (bear in mind that the legibility of a word can often be maintained even when only the first and last letters are recognizable)
2. Confident, fluid strokes
3. Consistent slant, sizing, scale, and intelligent spacing of letters
4. Uniqueness and personal touches; character

We can further elucidate this concept by turning our question on its head and asking, "What makes a signature bad?"

Again, there are many approaches to answering this question. Let's begin with one of the more obvious factors: generally poor handwriting. This, in turn, can have its root causes in a variety of issues; namely, making a habit of a flawed grip, posture, and paper placement in our formative years. Many of us have unfortunately committed many bad practices to muscle memory, as a result of receiving basic, uniformed, or even poor instruction early on. Indeed, as we continue to type more and write by hand less, handwriting instruction is increasingly de-emphasized as part of our education. And yet, we must hand-sign receipts, documents, holiday or event cards, etc. on a weekly, if not daily, basis.

Furthermore, as discussed in the preface, there is an impact from today's common "talent is innate" philosophy. A child who fails, at first, to produce beautiful letters is often unintentionally encouraged to continue failing. Well-meaning friends, family, and mentors choose to emphasize a child's other talents (you're so good at [insert skill here]; this just isn't your thing!"), but, instead, end up constructing solid arguments for giving up. Thus, many of us produced the best signature we could during our early teenage years, and have not attempted to improve or change it since.

Poor handwriting is an obvious issue in signature writing, but, paradoxically, another common cause of uninspiring signatures is when we learn the practice alphabet we were taught in our early years *too well* – never departing from it to personalize our letters. This tends to make our signatures look childish – simple reproductions of the models we were taught, with no display of mastery or flourish of our own. Whereas shoddy handwriting is a technical flaw, this is a flaw of design.

A multitude of resources exist to correct for (or avoid) technical issues in your overall handwriting, or to learn the principles of design. In this book, we will pull knowledge, tools, and techniques from several different disciplines and wield them with a laser focus to help you create and learn to sign a signature you love. In this way, you'll get to take the shortest path to the best result, while building a foundation in overall penmanship and design. Perhaps most importantly of all, you'll learn how to think and practice like an artist.

Our approach involves three main phases.

Phase One: Essential Knowledge
- How to make progress easy and permanent by managing mindset, dealing with mistakes, and cultivating practice as a habit
- Effective self-critique, and the difference between analytical and physical writing practice
- Overview of proper setup and tools

Phase Two: Design
- Fundamentals of signature design
- Assessing your current signature
- Reworking your design by:
  · Designing statement capitals
  · Refining control, fluency, and speed in minuscules
  · Leveraging scale, flourishing, and personal touches

Phase Three: Execution
- Making it happen with a practice program designed to integrate everything you've learned
- Customizing practice sessions for quick, quality improvements

How to Use This Book

 Everything should be made as simple as it can be, but not simpler.

— Albert Einstein

Wreck It

This is an art book! You'll be asked to tear or cut out pages, write notes inside of it, and fill up the workbook with your imperfect, Bambi-standing-up-for-the-first-time penmanship. Making mistakes is a fixed feature of making marks on paper, and making your mark is what this book is all about. Dispense with any ideas about keeping this book in pristine condition up front and commit instead to making a mess and having fun.

Skip Info and Exercises You Don't Need

Signature improvement is different for everyone, depending on the knowledge, fluency, and dexterity you begin with. This guide has been designed so that you can easily identify what kind of help you need and skip over information and drills that won't be of use to you. For example, if you already have beautiful cursive and a confident hand, you can skip most of the exercises that deal with improving fine motor skills and focus on adding attractive design elements and personalization to your existing signature. On the other hand, if you have never formally learned cursive or have not attained a satisfactory mastery of it, you may find these sections most helpful. What's more, if you intend to pursue penmanship at a higher level later on, the information on correct writing setup, grip/posture retraining techniques, and how to structure your practice sessions will prove invaluable.

Keep an open mind, but give yourself permission to decide what to focus on and what to ignore.

Practice Consistently

At this point I have to impart some rather unfortunate, but potentially liberating, information: fine motor skills are perishable.

This is unfortunate because it means that progress you've made can begin to slip away if you neglect to practice for several days in a row. At the same time, this information is liberating because mere awareness of it can prevent or cure moments of intense frustration. Say, for example, you knock out your first three days of practice exercises, and you notice a great improvement in your skill. If you are unable to practice for another three to four days, you may find upon your return that your skill seems to have reset almost to the starting point.

At times like these, remember that even professional penman often experience a similar deterioration of their skillsets after a vacation or other break from work, and must retrain their hands over the course of half a week or more to get back to project-appropriate skill levels. The feeling of frustration and disappointment that results is such a familiar companion to professionals that they've dubbed it "calligrapher's depression."

The good news is that your skills will typically return to you much more quickly than it took for you to initially acquire them. So when you find yourself face-to-face with a stark divide between what you feel you know how to do, or *should* be able to do, and what you actually *can* do, just remember that a little time is all that you need to get back on track.

Nothing we're going to do in this book is inherently complicated or difficult, but it does require a modicum of consistency until you really train your new signature into muscle memory. Odds are, you've been writing your signature the same way for years or even decades; this takes a little time to undo.

Try to begin your exercises at time when you'll be able to do them daily for five to seven days in a row. You don't have to spend more than 15 to 30 minutes per day, but the regularity of your practice is important, especially at the start. If you do have to take more than one or two days off in the midst of this, have patience with your hand when you get back to it – and remember that it might take a couple more practice sessions for your hand to snap back into shape.

Buddy Up!
There is an old adage in the creative world, espoused by many artists, designers, and innovators: "Don't design in a bubble." If you've ever successfully pursued

a creative endeavor, you may have already realized that attempting to be the student, the teacher, the creator, and the critic all at once often lends itself more to insanity than to real progress, let alone enjoyment.

You can exponentially increase both your chances of success and satisfaction throughout this process by choosing to pursue signature improvement with a friend or within a community, rather than in isolation.

Another proven (and fun) way to keep yourself on track is to attach stakes to meeting your goals. Make a bet with a friend that you'll finish this book by a certain date, or use a free tool like stickK (stickk.com), which allows you to set public or private goals and incentivize yourself to meet them. You can choose to tantalize yourself with a reward – like a nice dinner out or a day of lounging – or to keep yourself in line by setting consequences for not following through – a donation to a charity you don't believe in, grounding yourself for the weekend; the possibilities are limited only by your imagination.

Setting a clear goal, sharing it with people you respect, and adding stakes have all been shown to drastically increase success rates across a wide range of commitment areas, from weight loss, to developing creative habits, to starting a business. So commit to doing this with a friend or spouse, find a meetup, or join an online community where you can share your progress. Reddit.com and Instagram are treasure troves of inspiring content and great resources for engaging with like-minded communities. Head over to Instagram or Reddit and search terms like "Handwriting," "Penmanship," and "Calligraphy" for help keeping your momentum strong. Remember that any accomplished penman you come across will have worked hard to attain their "perfect" writing; avoid value comparisons where you label your work as "bad" and the work of others as "good." Inspiration can turn into frustration if you unfairly compare your first attempts at a new signature with the finely-honed writing of professionals who have logged hundreds or thousands of hours of practice.

However you choose to engage with others in your creative practice, just "don't design in a bubble."

Legal Implications of Signature Change

You may be wondering about the legal implications of changing the way you sign official documents, and you may see this topic discussed with varying degrees of authority and diligence online. I offer this section to provide an overview of the issue, pulling information from a variety of quality sources. However, I am not a lawyer, and nothing contained herein constitutes legal advice. Any legal decisions should be made with the guidance of your attorney.

Common sense tells us that signatures can change throughout our lifetimes for a variety of reasons, ranging from handwriting improvement or deterioration over time, to injuries that drastically change signing ability. A signature is a unique mark used to represent your intent and to identify you, and there are no rules about how this mark must look – or even that you must sign your name. Indeed, a signature could be as simple as writing an "X." Additionally, there is no formal process for legally changing your signature.

So what are the important considerations if you decide to alter the signature you use for legal documents?

In an article for Forbes.com entitled *New Treasury Secretary Lew To Change His Loopy Signature: Should You Too?*, practicing lawyer Robert W. Wood explains that, while there is no formal process for legally changing your signature "... consistency is what counts.... The norm is to do some commonsense conforming. That way key documents all match, including your driver's license, passport, etc. That means a trip to the DMV for a new license, applying for a new passport, and so on. Bank signature cards should be changed too, credit cards, and perhaps other documents."

If this seems like too much hassle or concerns you in any way, remember that it is by no means necessary that you change your legal signature as part of your signature redesign process. Most personal, and many professional, communications can be signed in any manner you choose, without fear of legal repercussions. One especially fun way to use your new signature is to digitize it for use on your blog, website, or email "signature block."

The Elements of Effective Practice

Mindset and Physiological State

> 66 *Basically, there are two parts in each person's brain: the upper-level logical part, and the lower-level emotional part. I call these the 'two yous.' They fight for control of each person. How that conflict is managed is the most important driver of our behaviors.* 99
>
> — Ray Dalio (billionaire investor and founder of Bridgewater Capital), *Principles*

> 66 *Whatever you feel or think, your exact state at the exact moment of your brush touching the canvas is in some way registered in that stroke. If there is interesting or reasonable sequence in your thoughts and feelings, if there is order in your progressive states of being as the paint is applied, this will show, and nothing in the world can help it from showing.* 99
>
> — Robert Henri, *The Art Spirit*

We often treat our emotional experience and our physiological state (the way our body feels) as secondary, or even unrelated, aspects of completing the task at hand. In reality, it would be almost impossible to overstate the impact of our emotional, mental, and physiological states on performance, learning, and the path to mastery. In clear acknowledgment of this truth, athletes and top-tier performers across many fields consider techniques like visualization and meditation to be integral components of their training routines.

I introduce this concept with some hesitation. I've been a skeptic as long as I can remember, always interested, but wary, of anything lacking in clear scientific evidence, logical basis, or anything with a general aura of "hokey-ness." Five or ten years ago, I was essentially dismissive of meditation, and anything else that seemed to prioritize emotional or mental well-being over logical thought and the pursuit of objective truth. I'm embarrassed to admit that I often thought of such practices as indulgences and wastes of time.

Several years ago, I began stumbling across information which made me suspect that I had made a grave mistake in the construction of this world view. In the time since, I have learned that human beings are first, and primarily, emotional creatures, and that our rationality – while still of paramount importance – is far less influential on our decision making, performance, and the mental chatter and self-talk that forms the basis of our relationships with ourselves. There is a mountain of rigorous psychological, biological, and evolutionary evidence to support this.

It's far beyond the scope of this book to enter into a deep discussion of these concepts. I propose only that you keep an open mind and give state management a try, especially if you suffer (as I did) from any amount of insecurity, apprehension, or from a loud inner critic when you write by hand.

I have often included short mental exercises or meditations prior to your actual writing exercises. It may be tempting to skip these. Don't do it! I promise that you will improve more quickly *and* enjoy this process significantly more if you give proper attention to your state prior to practicing. With the right mindset and a relaxed, intent physiology, writing practice can become a wonderfully meditative and cathartic process in its own right. With the wrong mindset and a tense, nervous, or impatient physiology, it's a chore which you will tire of quickly. Spend a couple of minutes priming yourself for success before you practice; you won't regret it.

If you still have doubts, or would like to know where to start looking for more proof, consider the following:

1. Psychologist Daniel Kahneman won a Nobel prize for his decades of research with Economist Amos Tversky, which proved that human beings are *not* the essentially rational and objective creatures we often imagine ourselves to be. Instead, emotional and instinctive drivers inform our behavior and thinking to such an extent that we often just act emotionally, then construct logical stories to support our choices and explain our behavior after the fact.

2. The FBI's hostage negotiation strategies are built upon psychological concepts that make management of their adversaries' emotional states the primary focus in a crisis; they explicitly acknowledge the premise that humans are not fully rational actors and emotional state must be addressed before positive progress can be made.

3. Tim Ferriss, a successful entrepreneur and best-selling author, has interviewed over 300 athletes, businesspeople, actors, artists and others at the tops of their fields in his wildly successful podcast *The Tim Ferriss Show*. Over 80 percent of his interviewees practice some form of meditation to manage and regulate mental/emotional/physiological state.

There are many more excellent studies and fascinating books which discuss the impact of mental and physiological state on performance and persistence on the road to mastery – Tony Robbins's infamous *Personal Power* program, *Drive* by Daniel Pink, and *Daring Greatly* by Brené Brown are just three wonderful, and very different, examples – but most of us have enough evidence within our own personal experience to be convinced. Take a few moments to answer the following questions as a thought exercise (or, better yet, as a quick journal exercise), and consider for yourself.

1. Think of a time in your life when you performed poorly. It could be in any arena – from an argument with a friend or family member, to a failure at school or work, to something as simple as losing a board game. Make the memory vivid in your mind. Try to remember how your body felt and what your mental state was like leading up to, and during, the poor performance. What did your body feel like? Was there tension in your neck, your chest, maybe your arms and legs? Was there a pit in your stomach? What were your heartbeat and breathing like? What kind of thoughts were going through your head – were they negative or positive?

2. Now think of a time when you felt incredibly successful – like you were performing at your best. Perhaps you were playing sports, or delivering a presentation you worked hard on, or perhaps you experienced a wave of creativity and inspiration as you worked through a problem or created something. Bring as many details to mind as you can. Where were you? What were you wearing? Who were you with? Now, remember how you felt. How were you breathing? What was your body language like? What level of focus and mental clarity did you have? What were your thoughts like?

Most people will immediately recognize a high correlation between their mental and emotional states and their performance. In fact, you may even find it difficult to come up with an example of a time when you were in a negative state and managed to perform well (or, certainly, to enjoy your task), or when you were in a positive or peak state but performed poorly. One of the greatest keys to cultivating consistently high performance is to recognize that you can manage your physiological and mental states, and to learn how.

As you go through this book, try to continue developing your awareness of your mental and physiological states, and how they impact your practice. Compare your work from a day when you were feeling great to your work from a day when you were feeling tired, rushed, or frustrated. Awareness in itself is valuable, but the benefits you'll gain from learning to manage your state better are priceless.

After all, in the same way that these techniques and principles apply to signature writing, they apply to everything else.

Mistakes and the "Beautiful Workbook Complex"

66 *...the greater the loss behind me, the greater the pride I may take in the price I have paid for that I love. Then the wreckage will not become a funeral mount above me, but will serve as a height I have climbed to attain a wider field of vision.* 99

— Ayn Rand, *Atlas Shrugged*

66 *Most of my sketchbooks are just scratch.* 99

— Brandon Rike (Graphic Designer and creator of branded artwork for blink-182, Pearl Jam, Ed Sheeran, and more), *Simple Methods for Custom Lettering*

If you're anything like me, you've probably spent considerable time jealously eyeing gorgeous signatures, calligraphy, and notebooks or journals filled with impossibly perfect script. With the help of images like these, you have fantasized about transforming your own signature into something truly outstanding. I want to commend you for your imagination and ambition, and to assure you that it can be done, but I also want to warn you: the process will not be that pretty.

Many of us, appreciating beautiful penmanship, are inspired to try our hands at it. But a problem arises when we enter into our practice envisioning clean, crisp workbook pages, filled with elegant practice letters which start out beautiful and become more beautiful. We make it very difficult to even begin when we worry about "ruining" our journals or workbooks with our unpracticed hands.

We also make it very difficult to enjoy the process of learning. I have affectionately dubbed this preoccupation with perfection the "Beautiful Workbook Complex."

The Beautiful Workbook Complex represents an extremely common, but highly romanticized notion of the process of learning something new.

Take a moment to evaluate your standards for your practice work and dispense with any that limit or restrict your right to make mistakes. In case you are unpracticed in the purposeful management of your expectations, let me help: you will produce many, many ugly letters. You will likely smudge, wrinkle, and otherwise foul up your practice pages.

I tell you this not to discourage you or to temper your enthusiasm, but simply to take the sting out of this truth. When you make your first marks on that first workbook page and don't like some of what you see, I want you to feel that you've accomplished the first step on the path to success – not that you've failed at the outset.

You are going to gather new design elements throughout this book, then combine them with your own personal flair to produce an original signature. This is a creative process which requires not just copying, but experimentation and invention. It also requires mistakes.

Try to reorient your perspective such that, each time you see your messy, error-filled practice pages, you feel pride in your persistence and improvement, rather than shame about your starting point or discouragement about your ability. Adjusting your attitude in this manner is not always an easy task – you'll need to remind yourself repeatedly to return to this outlook if you are accustomed to being hard on yourself – but if you can do it, you'll eliminate hours of unnecessary frustration, improve more quickly, and enjoy learning.

So, though you might be tempted, don't hide away or dispose of your early practice pages as though they are shameful evidence of your ineptitude – they aren't. They are evidence that you are learning something new. Plus, it's incredibly easy to misremember your starting point once you begin making progress. If you hit a plateau in your practice, it can be extremely heartening to look back and see how far you've already come.

I experienced this myself, when I redesigned my own signature. About 75 percent of the way through, I became convinced that I wasn't making real progress and that I'd never really get my signature to look how I wanted it. By chance, at the end of that practice session I happened to knock open my notebook to some of my earliest pages of practice. I was, quite frankly, blown away by the difference between my starting point and my current work – I had been utterly convinced that there was little change only moments before. Just like that, my frustration evaporated and my optimism returned.

If you're apprehensive about putting pen to paper, don't let yourself invent reasons to avoid getting started ("Maybe I should wait to start until I have a bunch of special pens, or until I rearrange my desk so I can sit perfectly") or try to force yourself through it. Instead, make it easier to be successful by asking yourself, "How can I make this fun? What if my goal was just to begin?"

The Role of Tracing in Practice

66 *He thinks of failure like learning to ride a bike; it isn't conceivable that you would learn to do this without making mistakes – without toppling over a few times. 'Get a bike that's as low to the ground as you can find, put on elbow and knee pads so you're not afraid of falling, and GO,' he says.* 99

– Ed Catmull, President of Pixar, on Andrew Stanton, writer/
director of *A Bug's Life, Finding Nemo,* and *WALL-E*

66 *If you want to lower your fear level, lower the danger level.* 99

– Barbara Sher, *Refuse to Choose!*

For most of us, in our typical, everyday use of handwriting, everything is automated. Whether our handwriting is good or bad, we don't have to actively think about how to form each letter as we write – we have internalized the movement required for each shape, and we simply reproduce it over and over again by habit.

However, when you first begin your signature improvement exercises, you may feel almost like you are drawing, rather than writing. This is because in order to produce these unfamiliar letterforms and/or flourishes, you must first correctly perceive them and then correctly reproduce them on paper. This requires engagement of your visual skills and your motor skills, the coordination of which is referred to as Visual-Motor Integration - a skill which is also highly important to drawing. The bigger the difference between your new signature design and your current signature (and current handwriting), and the more ornamentation you decide to use, the more your Visual-Motor Integration will be challenged.

Any time you find yourself having trouble getting started on your exercises, freezing up, or hitting a plateau, tracing can be a great tool for breaking through and creating momentum in your practice. Especially at the start, those blank workbook pages can be intimidating. Like the small bike and protective gear in the analogy from the Pixar luminaries above, tracing is an easy, immediate way to lower the stakes and get your pen to paper.

At times, I will explicitly recommend tracing exercises (usually when you first begin practicing a new letter), but remember that you can use your discretion and return to tracing anytime you feel stuck. You may even choose to make it a standard part of your warmup process. I recommend Staedtler brand 100% Rag Vellum (available on Amazon) for tracing exercises, because it is one of the few tracing papers that interacts well with pen ink. For a cheaper alternative, standard copier paper is lightweight enough that – with good lighting – it can usually be used for tracing without too much difficulty.

Tracing exercises are used widely in occupational therapy and other handwriting improvement courses to help students practice fine motor skills, get the feel of letterforms, and to internalize correct movements. By contrast, tracing has a bit of a stigma in many artistic disciplines. Indeed, many artists would tell you that tracing is a great idea... if you want to become great at tracing, but that if you want to get good at drawing, you should practice drawing. For our purposes, we know that tracing can be a beneficial tool – but there is a salient point within that statement which is as relevant to us as it is to aspiring artists. Tracing is an inherently different activity from freehand writing, and if you rely upon it too heavily or without careful intention, you will develop the former skill and not the latter.

The key to using tracing effectively in your practice is to remain mindful. Stay present and notice the *feel* of the slant, the spacing, the shape, the size, the rhythm, etc. of your letters. You can keep most tracing exercises brief (usually a line or two of a given letter is plenty), and vary the speed of your tracing from slow to fast. What motions are required in your shoulder, arm, wrist, hand, and fingers in order to produce the shapes?

The Magic of Habit Formation

—

66 *Most of the choices we make each day may feel like the products of well-considered decision making, but they're not. They're habits.* 99
    – Charles Duhigg, *The Power of Habit: Why We Do What We Do in Life and Business*

A habit is formed when a sequence of:

Cue >> Behavior >> Reward

is repeated enough times that the pattern becomes automated. By "automated," we mean that it occurs without conscious choice or explicit thought on your part. This is not simply a quirk in your thought process; there is an actual neurological difference. When a pattern, or habit loop, is running, activity is taking place in the most primitive part of your brain (the brain stem) rather than in your "thinking" brain (the prefrontal cortex).

Why should you care? Because this means that you can end the internal struggle of procrastination of any given task, forever, by intentionally creating habits. Let's consider two scenarios:

SCENARIO #1
- You read this book, get excited to start the exercises, but make no concrete plan about when you'll set aside time to practice. You figure you'll fit it in when you can – probably tomorrow. In the morning, you're tired and you don't want to get up extra early to practice before work or school, so you decide to practice at lunch. When lunch comes, you're stressed or busy and you feel like you don't really have full time and attention to devote to practicing – plus, it'd be hard to write while you eat. You can just practice after work. But after work, you get home and you just want to relax. You think about practicing, but you just want to have dinner and watch some Netflix.

You feel guilty, but you put off practicing again. You've spent the whole day with it hovering over your head, but you haven't done anything. The next day, you repeat the process. Does any of this sound familiar?

SCENARIO #2

- You understand that you need to set aside about 30 minutes per day to practice your signature. You decide that, realistically, you'll be most willing and able to do this right after you return home from work. You decide exactly where writing practice will fit in to your after-work routine and visualize it (i.e. you picture yourself sitting down to the table right after you walk through the door, take your coat off, and feed the dog). You commit to that plan, preferably telling another person of your intention and attaching some stakes to ensure you follow through. After work, you're tired but you follow through. You reward yourself with a scoop of ice cream, a movie, or simply basking in the sheer bliss of having succeeded. But wait, there's more! After a while, coming home from work becomes your automatic cue to practice writing. You walk in the door, take off your coat, feed the dog, and head over to the table and sit down to write. You don't ask yourself whether you should, or have to, or come up with ways to put it off until later. You literally have no thoughts about it at all – you just do it, like driving hypnosis or brushing your teeth in the morning. No willpower required. Next, you realize you can apply this process to almost anything. You become amazing and conquer the world.

The important elements in converting your practice into a habit are to ensure a consistent cue and a real reward.

It helps a lot if you can practice at the same time every day, as the time itself (and its place in the sequence in your day) strengthens the power of the cue. For the same reason, it's wise to do your practice after another behavior that you already do habitually.

In terms of a reward, it can be as simple as taking a moment at the end of practice to pat yourself on the back for a job well-done (thus creating a sense of accomplishment and pride), or as explicit as eating a treat or buying yourself a little present when you're first trying to solidify the habit. Additionally, the more enjoyable you can make the act of practice itself, the more quickly it will become an automated behavior rather than a conscious choice. So, play some music, light a candle, brew some tea, and relish the time you're making for yourself to work on something you care about.

All this being said, remember to cultivate your practice habit in a way that is uniquely suited to *you*. If you work best first thing in the morning, in the middle of the day, or at 2:00am – embrace your funk and build your habit into your unique routine.

Analytical and Physical Practice

Perhaps one of the most important things you will learn in this book is how to develop a discerning eye, and to unemotionally critique your own work. Sitting down each day and plowing through sheet after sheet of writing exercises without setting specific goals or analyzing your progress means more work with less results. Unsurprisingly, this quickly leads to frustration.

Instead, make analyzing and critiquing your work standard, and distinct, parts of your writing exercises. To do this effectively, start each writing session with *one to two specific, attainable* goals in mind. Examples would be, "today I will work on improving the consistency of my slant" or "today I will work on improving the spacing of my letters." These goals are clear, realistic, and easy to evaluate.

It's admirable, and even advisable, to start a new endeavor with big goals in mind. But too often, we neglect to break these down into manageable pieces, and it restricts our growth. If your goal for this entire process is to create your "dream signature," that's great – but when you sit down to practice on any given day, make sure you can answer the following question:

How will I know if I've been successful *in this session?*

If you sit down to practice thinking only in generalities about how you are working toward producing a nebulously-defined "perfect" signature, or if your only concrete goal is to perfectly replicate one of the sample letters in this book on your first try, you'll most likely be disappointed in what you produce on any given day. You'll only see the ways in which your work doesn't measure up to your final vision, and you'll unintentionally ignore all your small steps of improvement.

Focus on meaningful progress, not perfection.

Once specific goals are identified, you've set the stage for a much more painless critique of your work. I recommend taking time out for analysis either at the end of each practice session (reviewing the work you did in that sitting), or at the start of each new session (reviewing the work from the session before). My favorite way is the latter, for two reasons. First, I tend to be hard on myself, and reviewing work from the prior day gives me a little bit of distance from it and therefore tends to feel less vulnerable for me – making it easier to be objective. Second, assessing your most recent work leads naturally into setting specific goals for the new session – i.e. if I notice in my analysis that I was really struggling to make a fluid "k" in my last session, I might decide that, today, I'm going to break down the letter into two parts, and practice making the loop of the "k" more polished and shapely before attempting to move smoothly through the whole letter again.

The other advantage of segmenting your practice into analytical and physical sections is that it can help to quiet the mental chatter that otherwise might take place while you're writing. Writing is a kinesthetic activity that requires controlled movement and hand-eye coordination, and, to some degree, you need to get out of your head while you're doing it. This doesn't mean you should zone out completely or let your mind wander indiscriminately, but it *does* mean you should silence your inner critic ("that 'k' sucked!" "I'll never be good at this"). Knowing you have another time devoted to analyzing your work can help free you up mentally while you're actually writing.

Another skill worth cultivating is to channel what mental chatter you do have toward a positive focus. In other words, if you must notice and think about the quality of your letters as you write, train yourself to notice when you do something correctly – not when you do something wrong.

In an interview with David Grimes, a professional designer, calligrapher, and gifted teacher, I asked what typically spurred the inflection points or breakthroughs in the progress of his calligraphy students. His answer is a poignant and succinct lesson not only for written arts, but on how to think about learning anything:

"A student starts and he's excited, and then everything he puts down is just bad – and he knows it's bad because he has the teacher's version or the book's version right next to him, but he doesn't really know how to do it better. And then eventually he'll find this one step – it's like the bottom step on a staircase – and he'll take that step up, and whatever that achievement was (maybe he does this portion of a stroke well, or he doesn't drop ink, or his nib doesn't catch), that becomes his favorite thing in the world. Now, all of a sudden, it's not just an achievement, it's a prideful piece of what he has accomplished. Maybe his writing is all still just as low quality as it was before, but now he has this thing that he is achieving, and he can see that he's achieving it, and he knows that he wants to keep achieving it. It makes it not so depressing to look at your work when you have this thing that you're excited about, and at least you can point at one thing and say, 'I'm doing this right.'"

You can intentionally push yourself toward a breakthrough by learning to de-emphasize the notice you take of the faults of your hand – at least while you're in the process of writing – and instead focus on what you're doing right, even if it's only one thing. This is a well-researched and proven technique in the field of behavioral psychology, a practical fact of life for creators and innovators everywhere, and the key to enjoying the process of learning.

I recommend a total practice time of about 30 minutes per day – approximately five minutes should go to state exercises (meditation or visualization), five minutes to goal setting and analytical practice, and the remaining 20 minutes will be your physical writing exercises.

We will begin the process of learning effective self-critique in earnest in the self-assessment section of this book, and I will remind you of it and further instruct you in it throughout all of your exercises. For now, it's enough to know that you need to do it with careful thought and intention, as part of your regular practice.

Setup and Tools

> 66 *It would be better if you were unconscious.* 99
>
> — Dwight Schrute, *The Office*

You will find many sources in the fields of penmanship, calligraphy, and handwriting improvement which recommend, or even insist upon, highly specific tools and materials for practice. Because our goal is to keep this process simple, and because, for practical reasons, you will need to be able to produce your new signature no matter what pen and paper you use or what position you sign it in, we will not place heavy emphasis on specific writing instruments or aids. You can absolutely successfully redesign and learn to execute your signature with plain white copier paper and whatever pens you have lying around your house. *Never let lack of certain tools or difficulty in constructing the "perfect" setup stop you from practicing.* Taking action is always your top priority, and you should never allow setup details to become a barrier to practice.

Bearing that in mind, intentional setup and tool selection can speed your progress and condition you for success in more challenging endeavors that you might wish to undertake in the future, like overall handwriting improvement or any kind of ornamental penmanship. It can also be really fun to play with office supplies.

Basic Materials and Setup

In general, as long as you are not experiencing pain or dramatically restricting your movements while writing, you should feel free to choose any pen, paper, and setup which make writing easy, enjoyable, and comfortable for you.

Still, if you want to really optimize your practice, tools can facilitate or impede your progress to some degree. When I first began oil painting, my instructor insisted that I use professional grade paints (rather than student grade, which are cheaper). The reason was that professional grade paints are typically higher quality and therefore easier to work with, thus eliminating one difficulty on the path to mastery. I will not recommend that you purchase anything expensive or fancy, but I will strongly suggest that you don't get in your own way by choosing tools that are inherently harder to work with.

To that end, consider the following tips.

PEN CHOICE

It's well worth it to spend a little bit of time experimenting with different pens to find one you love. Plus, having a small variety on hand will allow you to ensure that you can write your signature with any pen. You don't need anything pricey or special; just try out options from several of the various categories available:

- Ballpoint (try fine and wide points)
- Felt or Fiber Tip
- Gel (my all-time favorite is the Uni-Ball 207 Premier; it has the squishiest grip I've ever felt)
- Optional: Fountain [01]

You can find all of these, inexpensively, online or in any store that sells office supplies. The only exception is the fountain pen, which will tend to be slightly more expensive and harder to find.

You may be surprised how much a new pen can impact your writing – especially if you are left-handed, have grip issues (we will discuss this in more detail in the next section), or tend to clutch your writing utensils tightly. My own Kung-Fu grip and inclination to write with immense pressure was significantly improved, in very short order, when I started using a fountain pen with a wider, flatter barrel and free-flowing ink. This made it possible to write by hand for longer periods of time without pain or fatigue.

Note: If you are left-handed, you have the greatest opportunity to benefit by choosing a pen with ink that flows easily and dries quickly. Your pen will naturally come into contact with your paper at an angle different from that of right-handers, and you may find many issues alleviated by practicing on smooth paper with a pen that moves easily across it. I have found the Zebra Z-Grip Flight (ballpoint) and the Pentel EnerGel (gel pen) to be excellent options – both were originally recommended to me by an occupational therapist specializing in handwriting.

01

Stick with a nonflex round nib in fine or medium (I like the Lamy Safari Fountain Pen) if you choose to use a fountain pen. I advise against purchasing pens with flexible nibs for use with this book. These pens require a separate skillset to be used effectively, and we will not cover that information here.

PAPER CHOICE

Again, for tracing exercises, I recommend Staedtler Plain 100% Rag Vellum (16 lb.). For free worksheets which can be printed on your tracing paper, visit createasignature.com and sign up for the newsletter. I advise starting with the Phase One worksheets. Tracing paper tends to be thin, so make sure your printer is set to print only on one side. The Staedtler paper works well with most home printers, but make sure to check that your paper is compatible with your printer if you choose a different brand. For all remaining (non-tracing) exercises, you can write directly on the worksheets included in the end of this book.

WRITING SURFACE, POSTURE, AND LIGHTING

Again, simple: make sure your chair and table/desk are a comfortable height, and that your writing surface is smooth and well-lit, as shown below.

Your feet should be able to rest flat on the floor, your back should be straight, and you should lean forward toward the table by pivoting from the hips (rather than slumping over and resting excessive weight on your arms as you try to write).

Your forearms should rest on the table, with elbows bent at approximately 90 degrees. Your paper should be placed slightly to your right if you are right-handed, or slightly to your left if you are left-handed. Paper slant can be a matter of preference (and, as we will see later, can be also used as an aid to change the slant of your writing), but most people will find it easier to write with the paper on a slight slant. This setup increases your freedom of movement and is easier on your body in a variety of ways. Try your best to approximate the setup below.

PRO TIP

Marcus Carlini, an expert penman specializing in movement, suggests that if you find it difficult to achieve a fluid motion with your right hand, it may be that you are resting too heavily on your right forearm. Try moving your left foot slightly forward to help subtly shift more weight to your legs and your left forearm, which

Aerial View

will allow you to support your upper body better and take some of the pressure off your writing arm. Of course, if you are a left-hander, move your right foot slightly forward to get the same benefits.

The easiest way to ensure your writing surface is smooth is to keep several sheets (around 5-10 is fine) of paper underneath the one you're working on.

If you're right-handed, it's ideal to have light coming from the left (so that you don't cast shadows over your writing), or to have light coming from the right if you are left-handed.

Deeper Considerations

As we briefly discussed in the introduction, many of us received lacking or limited instruction in handwriting as children. In some cases, this results in inefficient and painful grips, posture, and wrist positions.

Grip, in particular, is one of the most difficult aspects of our writing to change because it gets so deeply ingrained and automated after many years of use. For this reason, it's worth repeating that if you're not experiencing pain while writing, it's not essential for you to retrain your grip. You can still improve your signature even if you have an imperfect grip.

Grip

If you are having pain, especially if you must write by hand on a regular basis for school or work, or plan to pursue a higher level of penmanship, you might consider seeing an occupational therapist (OT) or your doctor. An OT can give you a personalized assessment and make recommendations for corrections, though this can sometimes be expensive. I have experienced grip and wrist position issues myself, and will share some of my favorite resources for addressing these below. Please remember to rely on the advice of your doctor or other qualified professional for any serious issues.

Let's review correct grip and wrist position. Your pen should rest on the side of your middle finger, with your thumb and index finger holding it in place on their respective sides. They should be near each other, but not touching. The barrel of the pen should run back to lay somewhere in between the middle point of the webbing between your index finger and thumb, and the side of the top knuckle of your index finger. This angle will vary somewhat based on your anatomy and preference, but in general, your pen should not stick straight up and down or lay flat against the knuckle of your thumb.

You may find that your grip differs significantly from what is shown in the graphic to the left. If so, again refer to your comfort level as a benchmark for severity of any grip issues.

You should also assess the position of your wrist, the intensity of your grip on the pen, and the pressure you apply to the paper. In general, you want to have a relatively neutral (straight) wrist, a very gentle hold on the pen, and to rest the side of your pinky finger/outside edge of your hand lightly on the paper.

If you're having trouble assessing whether or not your grip is correct, it can be useful to take a photo or video of your hand/wrist while you're writing normally. Compare the result with the graphic to the left. What is the angle of your hand to the paper? The angle of your pen? How are your fingers placed?

If you find that you grip is close to correct, but you identify a couple of issues – for example, if your finger position looks good, but you're holding the pen too tightly and your wrist is bent at an awkward angle – it's worth it to try making those tweaks when you begin your signature writing practice. Try to approximate the setup shown on page 36 whenever you sit down to write, and reposition yourself or lighten your pressure whenever you catch yourself slipping out of proper form. You can make a lot of progress with minimal nuisance, and a better grip can help your signature and your overall handwriting.

On the other hand, if you find that your grip is drastically different from the example above, these are your two key takeaways:

1. Complete retraining of your grip is possible, but difficult. It's up to you to decide whether it is worth it. My recommendation is only to undertake it if you have pain and/or plan to pursue higher levels of penmanship or handwriting improvement. In most cases, you can still improve your signature without altering your grip – you can just follow all the exercises in this book with your normal hold and posture.

2. If you do have pain, *never* power through practice sessions or extended periods of writing. Regularly practicing through pain can lead to more serious issues, and it simply isn't worth damaging your hand and wrist (and your dominant ones, at that).

If you decide to retrain your grip, have patience with yourself. Try to approximate the correct grip shown above, and consider consulting an OT. You may experience a temporary decrease in control or deterioration of your writing skills when first experimenting with a new grip, due to simple unfamiliarity with how it feels and how it alters your flow of movement. This is to be expected; it's just a phase to work through. My all-time favorite recommendation for retraining grip, courtesy of Jan McKlesky, OT and creator of the *First Strokes* writing program, is to get an adult coloring book and practice your new grip while coloring. This is a fun, relaxing way to retrain your muscles.

In my case, I bought a package of cheap, triangular pencil grips on Amazon, put them on colored pencils and pens, and practiced on an adult coloring book I'd received for Christmas. This exercise doesn't require total focus; I often colored for just a few minutes while having my morning coffee, or while listening to an audio book, or chatting on the phone.

Remember that when starting to retrain your grip, success lies in *coming back* to the proper grip – not in maintaining it throughout the session. You'll start off intentionally holding your pen correctly and forcing a light touch, but as your mind wanders, your death-clutch or awkward hold will try to reassert itself. Each time you catch your hand in that act and move back to the correct position, that's a success. After some time, you'll find that your hand reverts back to its old ways less and less frequently, and your new grip begins to feel natural.

Optional Extras

There are a few more tools which are worth noting in this section. These can be purchased relatively economically, but are often also easy to access for free at school or work.

1. Dry erase [02] or chalk boards
   a. These can be surprisingly useful in two different ways:
      i. **when you're learning a new letter, especially if you're having particular difficulty.** It can be very illuminating to try reproducing the letter on a large scale. Suddenly, faults in your movement or construction of the letter, which may have been elusive before, will become very clear.
      ii. **when you are working to increase the speed of your signature.** The easy glide of a marker over a dry erase board preserves all the important motion, while eliminating the resistance caused by your arm resting against a table and your pen moving across paper. I was shocked by the impact of just one session of practice on a dry erase board on the overall speed and fluency of my signature on any surface.
2. Slanted desk
   a. Slanted desks come highly recommend from penmen and OTs alike. An angled writing surface forces you to write with less pressure on your writing arm – so this is of particular value if you've identified that you press too hard or squeeze your pen when you write. I found a slanted lap desk on Amazon (the Visual Edge slant board) which has a dry erase board surface – allowing me to reap the benefits of points #1 and #2 here simultaneously.
3. Pencil/Pen grips
   a. If you have some discomfort with your grip, consider getting a package of pencil grips which will fit many smaller-barreled pens. I like The Classics Triangle Pencil Grips and The Pencil Grip Original (both sold by The Pencil Grip and available on Amazon or most office stores).

02
———
Pro Tip: Don't have a dry erase board? Just get a dry erase marker and practice on your mirror."

Hypocrisy (Sort of)

Now that we've covered the ideal setup for the most efficient practice, I'd like to confess that, on several occasions, I have been guilty of practicing my signature on my small lap desk while sitting cross-legged on my couch and bingeing Netflix. If you do this habitually, your practice will be less efficient, and you may also end up committing sloppy movements to muscle memory. On the other hand, if you get overly fixated on details and use less-than-perfect circumstances as an excuse not to practice at all, you will make no progress and you will learn nothing. Things like posture, setup, and tools will become increasingly important if you choose to pursue other written arts, but for our purposes, use your judgment, do what it takes to get yourself to sit down and write, and be forgiving with yourself when your practice isn't perfect.

Whenever you find yourself resisting getting started, listing off excuses to postpone practice in your head, or otherwise procrastinating, try asking yourself the following two questions, which I learned from the works of world-famous performance coach Tony Robbins and best-selling author Tim Ferriss, respectively:

1.   What can I do with what I have right now?
2.   What would this look like if it were easy?

The answers to these questions will almost always yield ideas about how to move forward and take action, *immediately*, without making it feel like a chore. We often do ourselves a disservice in learning (and in life) when we enforce unnecessary rules upon ourselves. This section, and the recommendations in it, are intended to provide you with helpful information; don't make them into a set of prerequisites that must be met before any practice can take place.

Design Fundamentals and Technical Execution

In many fields, becoming an expert involves acquiring knowledge that the average person wouldn't have, recognize, or even understand. The layman typically can't participate in the discipline at the level of the expert. The paradox of learning design, on the other hand, is that you dedicate much of your time to learning explicitly what everyone knows intuitively.

What looks good to the untrained eye?

We know it when we see it; but to create it intentionally, we need an expanded awareness.

Human beings are highly visual creatures. Artists, photographers, and other creators study how elements like light, color, texture, and more affect their audiences. Skillful manipulation of these elements can evoke strong emotional, and even visceral, responses – allowing artists to make statements, pose questions, and connect with their audiences in subtle and fundamental ways. Art can cause us discomfort and angst, create states of harmony and peace, and everything in between.

People are hard-wired to look for patterns, we have a finely-tuned sense of visual balance [03] , and our eyes are drawn to contrast, movement, and incongruities. This is the subset of design elements which is most relevant to the written arts.

Understanding our drive to seek out patterns and balance, and our satisfaction in finding them, makes it easier to see why consistent, uniform letters lay the foundation for good signature design. It is only once we can create a series of

03

____

What is visual balance?

The terms we use to discuss this - "visual balance" and "visual weight" – are themselves excellent analogies for the experience we all go through when viewing a design.

We often use words like "heavier," "lighter," or "off-kilter" to describe two dimensional shapes and their placement within a given composition. What we really mean is that each element of a design exerts a different force of attraction – a sort of gravitational pull - over our eyes and our attention. We have an innate desire for all of those forces to reach a state of equilibrium within a design.

In signatures, or any written art, we are most commonly pursuing asymmetrical balance. This means that elements which are dissimilar to each other in terms of size, shape, position, direction, etc. (in other words, elements with different visual weights) are organized in such a way that they balance each other out when the design is taken in as a whole.

As you look through the signature samples below, and begin to reimagine your own signature design, ask yourself – if this signature were set atop a fulcrum, would one side weigh the other down?

shapes which seem to belong together, that we can add in delightful flourishes or embellishments which break our pattern and draw the eye in an intelligent way.

In penmanship and calligraphy, there are many established "hands" (complete alphabets, number and punctuation sets, written in very specific styles and according to specific rules), such as Copperplate, Spencerian, and Engrosser's Script. These hands are almost invariably built upon one to three "parent" letters, usually "i," "n," "o," "l," and "j" which prescribe the shape of the curves, the angle of lines, and the space occupied by every other letter in the alphabet. In other words, almost every impressively styled alphabet in existence is constructed with only a handful of simple shapes which are repeated over and over again in different combinations.

This is why, in our exercises, we'll focus first on refining our hands, and then on adding impressive flourishes.

Problems with technical execution interfere severely with our ability to create an attractive signature. Issues such as poorly formed letters, unintentional variation between letterforms, inconsistent alignment to the baseline, inconsistent slant, sizing, and spacing are common culprits which seem to make the observer's eye bounce around everywhere, and nowhere, at the same time.

For clarity, let's consider this example of my original signature bellow, which suffered from each and every one of these flaws.

Original Signature

Anyone who looks at this signature can easily tell us that it's "bad." But we want to be able to identify *why* we don't like it so that we can work strategically to change it. Let's take an even closer look:

1. Poorly formed letters: particularly, look at the "k" and "e" (the last two letters of my first name). They are written so sloppily that both are essentially just

straight vertical lines. Also consider the "a" at the end of my last name. It has a retracing error (the slight loop that was created at the upper left where I transitioned from the "g" to the "a" and failed to retrace carefully) as well as an incomplete closure; the lines don't meet at the top, leaving the "a" open.

2. Variation between letterforms: look at the two "o's" in my first name. The first is relatively round, upright, and small. The second is about 50 percent larger, pointy, has a retracing error, and seems tilted to the right. You can see a similar variation between the "e" in my first name and my last name.

3. Inconsistent alignment to the baseline: look at the bottoms of each of my letters, and how they align (or don't align) with each other. Some float upwards, while others drift below the imaginary baseline.

4. Inconsistent slant, sizing, and spacing: some of the letters in my name are straight upright, some lean to the right, and some even lean slightly left. We already discussed the sizing issues with the two "o's," but we can see another sizing issue in the "k" and the "g." The descender of the "g" is stubby and cramped, while the ascender of the "k" is comparatively tall and thin. Ideally, these two elements would be similar in height and shape, creating a nice sense of balance with each other. In terms of spacing, look at how crowded the letters "roo" of my first name are. Compare that to the space between the "Ve" of my last name, and the gaping space between my first and my last name.

These are all issues of technical execution.

In terms of design, this signature was almost completely bereft of any stylistic elements. The "B" looks the way it does because, when I started signing my name, I attempted to copy how my mother signed the "B" in her name, and the habit stuck. When I got married and had to learn to sign my new last name (Vega), I tried to make the "V" fancy by adding that little stick in the upper left of the letter. The rest of the signature is simply a result of me trying to write quickly in cursive (when my cursive was sloppy even when I wrote slowly) and then ingraining those jerky, incorrect movements into muscle memory over the course of many years.

Let's look at some samples of well-designed, well-executed signatures. Review each one yourself and try to recognize how it employs the principles of good design that we've discussed in this section and in the introduction.

Consider:

- How legible is it?
- Do the strokes look confident and fluid?
- How consistent are the slant, sizing, scale, and spacing of the letters?
- What personal touches/flourishes are there? Is there a clear personality to the writing? How do you know?
- What patterns can you find in the writing? Are certain design elements repeated throughout it?
- Does the overall design convey a sense of visual balance?
- Are there any "delightful contrasts" within the design? Is the signature "breaking the rules" in any way?

On Graphology

———

There is an entire area of knowledge, called graphology, which is dedicated to making inferences about the personality, intentions, and sometimes even predicting the future of individuals based on analysis of their handwriting.

Graphologists assert that certain human traits or tendencies will present themselves consistently via the same handwriting characteristics – i.e. the size, shape, and slant of your writing all indicate something about your personality. It is also commonly claimed that changing certain aspects of your writing will, in turn, change the corresponding aspects of your personality. For example, having a signature where all or part of your name appears to be "crossed out" is considered to be a sign of low self-esteem, or even a warning sign of suicide.

While I do believe (as many artists do) that your emotional/physiological state will impact your strokes and the overall look of your writing, I find much of the literature on graphology to be plagued by pseudoscience and plain misinformation. As such, we will not cover it extensively in this book.

My recommendation is to abide by a simple rule: if the way you're writing your signature generally makes you feel good while you write it – you're going to be okay.

If you're signing your name over and over while experiencing any negative emotions, I would recommend making some changes. There is a strong neurobiological case to be made that, if this is your habit, signing your name could eventually become a trigger for those negative emotions.

If you're still concerned, there is a wealth of free, easily understood information online. Just search "graphology" or "handwriting analysis."

Signatures

Stephen Kerry

Oskar Attar

Feng Suave

Sophia Johnson

Thomas Herzberg

Nicole Fratton

Signatures

Phillip Pratt

G. Anthony

Alex Tuffy

Celina Colton

L. Jhaine

Orlando Gomez

Now let's review some of these design concepts together.

The twelve signature samples above showcase a wide range of variety in style and personality, but every single one has a relatively high level of legibility, was written in a confident, fluid hand, and displays a strong coherency of letterforms. These first three points from our list of considerations are met by this set of samples almost as a prerequisite.

What did you note about how flourishes are used, or how personality is conveyed? When talking about flourishes, in addition to noticing what attributes are common, it's equally important to notice what's *not* present. Even the most complex signatures among this set restrict themselves to only a few flourishes, and the majority of them are a testament to how great design can be achieved through solid technical execution and strategic, minimal embellishments. We'll talk about this in greater depth as you work through your own signature redesign.

Patterns and visual balance are, perhaps, the most interesting topics to discuss here. The simplest pattern that can be seen here is the use of statement capitals. Indeed, the first two signatures – Stephen Kerry and Oskar Attar – achieve a polished look by pairing large, swooping capitals with clean, tidy minuscules and hardly any other flourishes.

The Phillip Pratt, L. Jhaine, and Orlando Gomez signatures make their impact in a similar way, but with the added element of creating interesting relationships between letters. The way the curve of the first "P" in Phillip Pratt is extended to form the curve of the second and third "p's" in the name is not only a sleek design detail, but a time-saver as well. I particularly love how the "J" and "h" echo the shape of the "L" in L. Jhaine, and how the "O" and the "G" in Orlando Gomez are mirror images of each other. Each of these letters is quite simply done, but the patterns within them, and the way they interact with each other, make for signatures with layered inspiration.

The Thomas Herzberg, Nicole Fratton, Celina Colton, and Alex Tuffy signatures are all designed around stark, extended lines that repeat throughout the names. It's interesting to see how varied the effect of these lines can be when the angle, length, and number of lines is changed, and paired with different styles of handwriting.

What can we notice about visual balance? Look at the signatures that have embellishments toward the beginning of the name. These signatures almost always have an extended exit stroke or a flourished final letter that helps balance the visual "weight" of the design. G. Anthony, Feng Suave, and Alex Tuffy are especially good examples.

Finally, what rule-breaking or delightful contrasts can be found? In this set of examples, Sophia Johnson and Alex Tuffy are the rock stars of misconduct and juxtaposition. We'll discuss this in more detail in the flourishing section, but – generally speaking – it is not a good idea to have many lines which cross over each other in your signature. For one thing, it can make it take forever to write your name, and it also tends to lead to a messy or ridiculous looking design. However, in the Sophia Johnson example, each line is placed so well that the initials are heavily emphasized *and* the entire name is still legible. The extreme variation in size between the capitals and minuscules is also a deft use of contrast.

Alex Tuffy stretches the boundaries of legibility and consistent letterforms but pulls it off by leaning into the contrast and pairing the loose, undisciplined minuscules with clean, angular capitals. The similar length of the extended strokes on the "A," "T," and the "y," and their nearly equal spacing create a perfect sense of balance and counteract any cohesion lost by the mischievous minuscules.

For even more inspiration, check out our curated Pinterest board at https://www.pinterest.com/coolsignatures/signature-inspo/, or search the board "Signature Inspo" by CoolSignatures. A quick Google search will also yield many useful results.

What If You *Want* an Illegible Signature?
Some signatures look good even though they can't be easily read. They are typically either purposefully abstract, like the "A. Morgen" signature to the right, or the product of a disciplined hand writing a familiar pattern at speed, like the "Ben Cabrera" example.

At their best, illegible signatures tell the story of a well-disciplined hand calmly, smoothly, almost carelessly laying down the strokes.

A. Morgen   Ben Cabrera

I once saw a woman Salsa dancing at a club in Spain. She was on the floor song after song, moving flawlessly through step after complex step – but the thing that struck me about her was how bored she looked. Her face was relaxed, her eyes wandered nonchalantly, and she didn't seem to even be breaking a sweat – when all the while her feet kept time perfectly with the music. It was the result of a casual grace, earned through years of practice, applied effortlessly to a task that had become easy. No wasted movement, no missteps, no self-doubt.

The really attractive illegible signatures are just like this. The reason they seem to convey an enviable sense of motion, a suggestion of perfect letters, a vestige of impeccable design, is that all of these things do indeed lay behind the mark. Unfortunately, this can mean that mastering a truly inspired abstract signature is (somewhat counterintuitively) more work than mastering an excellent signature with more legibility.

When you're done with the practice exercises in this book, if you continue to use your new signature on a regular basis in a variety of situations, it's likely that it will eventually relax and slip toward illegibility if you let it. If you want to shortcut this process and intentionally work toward illegibility, there are a few things to think about:

- Minuscules tend to get extremely small
- Capitals get very large
- Space between letters increases
- Flourishes are minimal
- Strokes are done with fast, confident motion

Take note of these characteristics – you can use them during your signature design mockup exercise later if you want to work toward an illegible signature.

Starting Assessment

❝ *All the fault is hers; hers is all the glory.* ❞

— Johann Wolfgang von Goethe, *Nature*

You may be tempted to skip this section for a variety of reasons – perhaps you feel you already have a good enough sense of where you are, and you're eager to move beyond it. Perhaps, like I did, you hate your current signature so much, you don't want to create another physical record of it. Or, perhaps you already like your signature, and you just want to design a new, fancier version for fun.

Whatever your skill level or sentiments about your current signature, I encourage you to start your redesign with an initial assessment. It is highly valuable both to have a record of your starting point, and to use your existing signature to inform your choices about what to change and what to preserve as you redesign.

So, without further ado, please sign your name at least three times below. Sign the way you normally do, with your usual grip, posture, speed, etc. [Note: if you never learned cursive, you can print your name below – the assessment that follows will still be relevant.]

Sign your name

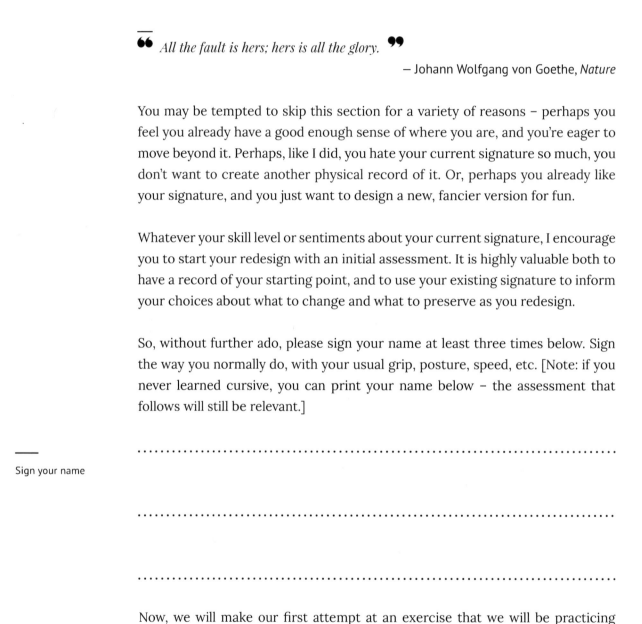

Now, we will make our first attempt at an exercise that we will be practicing repeatedly throughout this book: evaluation without judgment.

Look at your signature and try to refrain from making broad value judgments like "it's good/bad/ugly/pretty/etc." Statements like these aren't useful to us because they give us almost no actionable information, and the negative ones do us an additional disservice by putting a damper on our emotional state and eroding our motivation. Instead, ask yourself the following questions, and be specific in your answers:

1. How is my current signature different from the signature I want?
2. What do I like about my current signature? (If your initial reaction to this question is "Nothing," push a little harder. Try asking yourself "If I really wanted to find something to like about my signature, what would it be?")

To answer the first question, it may help to look back at the signatures from the last section. Which ones do you like best? Why? How are they different from, or similar to, your current signature?

To answer the second question, let's revisit my starting signature:

Brook Vega — Original Signature

In the last section, we talked about all of its errors and undesirable qualities. Based solely on this, you might think that there wasn't anything about my signature that I wanted to preserve – but that isn't the case. I like:

• The exaggerated size of the capitals versus the minuscules
• The extended lead-in stroke of the capital "B"
• The general sense of roundness of the letters (at least the ones I wrote correctly) which is characteristic of my handwriting
• The relatively good legibility

Now, turn back to your own signature, and consider the following list of attributes. For each one, ask yourself "Do I want to change or preserve this aspect of my signature?" It's okay if you're unsure about the answers; you'll learn more about all of these elements as you work through this book, and you can change your mind at any time. Don't overthink this exercise – it's merely a starting point for identifying your tastes.

Feel free to make notes against each point for easy reference later.

- Choice of name (i.e. are you signing your full first and last name, first initial and last name, including a middle initial, etc.?)
- Overall letter sizing
- Size of capitals versus size of lowercase letters
- Scale of lowercase letters [04]
- Space between letters
- Space between first and last name
- Slant
- Roundness versus sharpness/angularity of letters
- Ornamentation/flourishes
- How letters join to one another
- Quality of strokes (fluidity, pressure, etc.)
- Consistency

04

———

Scale of Lowercase Letters

This refers to how tall the x-height, or middle line, of a letter is compared to the ascending or descending part of a letter. For example, if you have a lowercase "h" in your name, how tall is the "tail" of the "h" compared to the "hump?"

Design Your New Signature

As discussed in the introduction, we are going to break your signature redesign process down into three steps.

1. Designing statement capitals
2. Refining control, fluency, and speed in minuscules
3. Leveraging scale, flourishes, and personal touches to maximize design impact

At each stage, I will make recommendations to help you create an appealing design which is practical and easy to learn, but you will make choices guided mainly by your own preferences. Don't stress or linger at any design phase too long – you will not be permanently locked into anything you choose. Since we are creating your signature piece by piece, you won't be able to see *exactly* what the finished product looks like at the start. But the beauty of this process is that, as you begin to practice your new signature regularly, you will gain greater control, fluency, and confidence in your hand. This means that if you decide to change an element or two of your signature toward the end of the process, you'll find it much easier and quicker to integrate that into your design.

Step One: Designing Statement Capitals
In the pages that follow, you will find a diverse set of fonts for every letter of the alphabet – all in capitals. There are 52 different fonts for each letter. They were selected based on their variety/contrast to each other and how well they lend themselves to being reproduced by hand. We'll use these fonts as a starting point for redesigning the capital letters in your signature.

If you keep an open mind and remember that you always have the ability to further customize the capitals you choose, there is plenty in the following pages to inspire great statement capitals for any name. However, certain letters of the alphabet – "G" and "Q" for example – are more complex and varied by nature than simpler letters like "I," "C," or "L." As a result, you may notice that there is a more diverse range of options for certain letters. Don't despair – if your name(s) begin with capitals that lend themselves less to fanciness, you can always add drama and interest to your signature by playing with size/scale, and adding flourishes elsewhere in your name. There will be plenty of opportunity to do this later in the process.

However, if you don't fall in love with any of the examples provided, there are tons of additional resources online where you can get inspiration for your capitals. All the fonts in this book are sourced from Google Fonts, which has hundreds of additional fonts online. MyFonts.com and 1001freefonts.com are also good resources with a lot of variety. All three have features that allow you to easily customize the font preview – meaning you can see how your initials (or even your full name) look in hundreds of different fonts in seconds. You can also select certain font categories, like "Handwritten" or "Script" to ensure you're scrolling through the most relevant fonts for your purposes. If you go this route, print out your chosen capitals at an appropriate size for practice (the ones in this book are printed in size 32 fonts), then carry on with the workbook exercises normally.

Now, before you start perusing the fonts, there are a few practical matters to consider.

First, which name do you intend to sign? Will you sign your full first and last name, or include a middle initial? Some people choose to sign with their first initial and full last name. Do you have a suffix (Jr., Sr., etc.) after your name? Decide on how you'll sign so that you know how many (and which) capitals you need to choose from the sets of fonts below.

Next, how much do you care about aesthetics versus speed? To some degree, once you have trained your signature into muscle memory, it will automatically "simplify" itself by slightly deteriorating in terms of legibility and frills whenever you choose to write it quickly. However, if you choose highly ornamental capitals, these will almost always take longer to sign, and may look worse than simpler letters when you are forced to write quickly. In general, the less complex the letters, and the fewer number of times you have to lift your pen from the paper, the quicker you'll be able to write.

Finally, choosing model letters that share some characteristics with your natural handwriting will make the training process easier and the final product more authentic. For example, if your typical handwriting is generally upright and rounded, you'll have an easier time learning to sign new capitals that are also upright and rounded, rather than capitals with a dramatic slant and sharp shapes. This is a good time to refer back to the questions in the Starting Assessment section; which characteristics of your current signature did you identify that you like? Can you find capitals below that share some of those characteristics?

You can, of course, make a drastic change if you want to. You can learn to write with backwards, upright, and forward slants; large, round letters and tiny, spiky ones; tall, flowing ascenders and descenders and compact and tidy ones – just remember to set realistic expectations about practice. Your hand will often tend to revert back to your natural writing style, so significant changes may take more time to master. Remember also that some fonts will have letters with thick strokes and hairline strokes – this is not an effect you can create in a practical manner without use of a calligraphy pen. So focus on the overall shapes of letters, and not the variation in stroke weights.

Let's get started! Review the sets of fonts beginning on the next page and choose all the capitals you need for your signature. You do not need to choose the same font for both (or all) of your capitals, but you can if you want to. All fonts appear in the same order for each letter, so you can easily find the same font for all of your initials if you choose. There is also an index of fonts on page 170 for easy reference.

With the above considerations in mind, simply choose capitals that you like, and that you believe go well together. Make note of your choices by flagging, circling, or highlighting, **but don't mark up the letters themselves – you'll be using them for tracing exercises and as reference points later on.** Feel free to tear or cut out the pages with your chosen capitals so that you can keep them in plain view while working through the exercises later in this book.

A's

A A A A A A A A
A A A A A A A A
A A A A A A A A
A A A A A A A A
A A A A A A A A
A A A A

B's

B B B B B B B **B**

B B B B B B ß B

B B B B B B B B

B B D b B B B B

B B B B B B B B

B B B B B B B B

B B B B

C's

C C C C C C C C

C C C C C C C C

C C C C C C C C

C C C C C C C C

C C C C C C C C

C C C C C C C C

C C C C

D's

D D D D D D D D

D D D D D D D D

D D D D D D D D

D D D D D D D D

D D D D D D D D

D D D D D D D D

D D D D

E's

E E E E E E E
E E E E E E E
E E E E E E E
E E E E E E E
E E E E E E E
E E E E E E E
E E E E

F's

G's

G G G G G G G G

G G G G G G G G

G G G G G G G G

G G G G G G G G

G G G G G G G G

G G G G G G G G

G G G G

H's
_

H H H H H H H H

H H H H H H H H

H H H H H H H H

H H H H H H H H

H H H H H H H H

H H H H H H H H

H H H H

I's

I I I I I I I I

7 L I / I / I I

I I I I I I I 9

I I I / I 9 I 9

I I I I I I I I

I I I I I I I I

I I I I

J's

K'<u>s</u>

K K K K K K K K

K K K K K K K K

K K K K K K K K

K K K K K K K K

K K K K K K K K

K K K K K K K K

K K K K

L's

M'ₛ

M M M M M M M M m

M M M M M M M M M

M M M M M M M M M

M M M M M M M M M

M M M M M M M M M

M M M M M M M M M

M M M M M

N's
_

O's

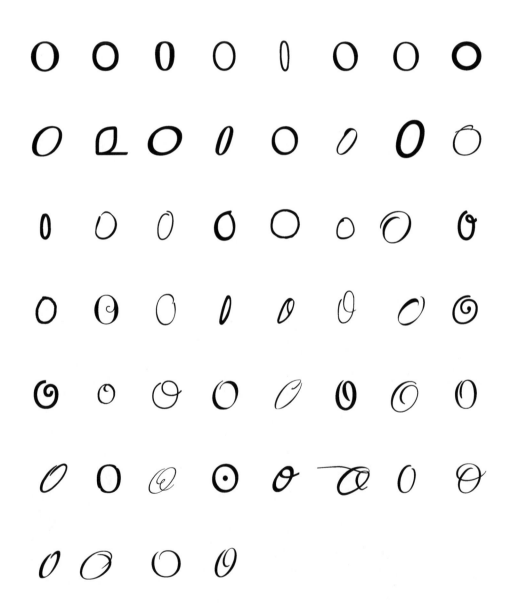

P'_s

P P P P P P P **P**

P P P P P P P P

P P P P P P P P

P P P P P P P P

P P P P P P P P

P P P P P P P P

P P P P

Q's

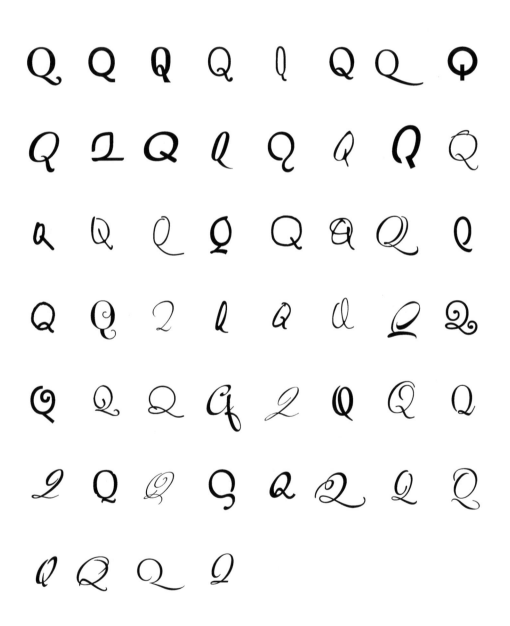

R's
_

R R R R R R R R

R R R R R R R R

R R R R R R R R

R R R R R R R R

R R R R R R R R

R R R R R R R R

R R R R

S's

S S S S S S S S

S S S S S S S S S

S S S S S S S S S

S S S S S S S S

S S S S S S S S

S S S S S S S S S

S S S S

T's

T T T T I T T T

T L T J T T T T

T T T T T T T T

T T T T T J T T

T T T T T T T T

T T T T T T T T

T T T T T

U's

U U U U U U U U

𝒰 U U U U ∪ **U** U

u u ∪ U U ∪ 𝒰 U

U U U U u u 𝒰 𝒰

U U U U 𝒰 U U U

𝒰 U 𝒰 U 𝒰 U U 𝒰

U 𝒰 U 𝒰

V's

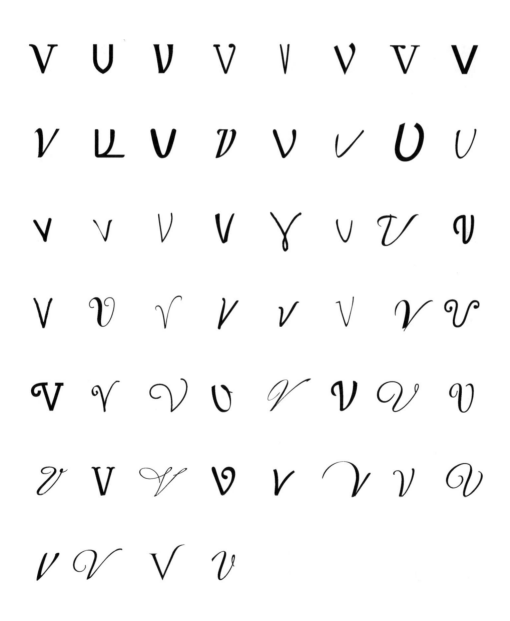

W's

W W W W W W W W

W W W W W W W W

W W W W W W W W W

W W W W W W W W

W W W W W W W W

W W W W W W W W

W W W W

X's

Y'ₛ

Y Y Y Y Y Y Y Y

Y Y Y Y Y Y Y Y

Y Y Y Y Y Y Y Y

Y Y Y Y Y Y Y Y

Y Y Y Y Y Y Y Y

Y Y Y Y Y Y Y Y

Y Y Y Y

Z's

Z Z Z Z Z Z Z **Z**

Z Z Z Z Z Z **Z** Z

z z z Z Z z Z z

Z Z Z Z z z Z Z

Z Z Z Z z z Z Z

Z Z Z Z Z z Z Z

Z Z Z Z

Step Two: Improving Legibility and Control in Minuscules

If the lowercase (minuscule) letters of your signature currently look childish, like illegible scribbles, or if you never learned cursive at all, this section is of paramount importance.

This section is intended to help you refine your minuscules by improving your fine motor control, confidence, and the legibility of your letters; it is not truly a "design" step in the sense that the Statement Capitals and Flourishing steps are.

To refine your minuscules, we'll be doing drills using the practice alphabet below. This alphabet has been specially crafted to be basic, impersonal, and easy to trace and learn. Once you begin your exercises, you'll focus specifically on mastering the letters that appear in the lowercase portion of your signature (versus attempting to learn the entire alphabet). This will help you to improve the consistency of the size, shape, and slant of your letters – providing a solid foundation for your signature design. After some time, you will abandon the practice alphabet and allow the personality of your natural hand to creep back in, augmented by the gain in your fine motor skill ability.

This means that you don't want to learn the letters from this alphabet "too well." Your goal is to improve control and fluency in your own, unique script – not to be able to perfectly reproduce the model letters. This will happen organically, if you let it.

You have two different sizes of letters here to choose from. When you begin your practice exercises, begin working with the size that mostly closely resembles your natural handwriting - or (if different) the size that is closest to how large or small you want the letters in your final signature to be.

Please take note, as you look over this practice alphabet, that there are four letters which are considered "semi-extended" – "d," "p," "q," and "t." Each of these letters either rises above the x-height or below the baseline but has a somewhat shorter height or length than the other letters with ascenders or descenders. It is important to notice this when you begin practicing.

abcdefghijklmnopqrstuvwxyz

the quick brown fox jumps
over the lazy dog

a b c d e f
g h i j k l
m n o p q r s t
u v w x y z

a b c d e f
g h i j k l
m n o p q r s t
u v w x y z

Minuscule Practice Alphabet

Remember, the lowercase letters in your final signature won't look like the model letters here because:

1. You'll relax back into the natural personality of your writing as time goes on.
2. You're going to add flourishes and play with size and scale later on.

That said, if you strongly prefer to choose a different alphabet to work with, you can take the same steps we discussed in the Statement Capitals section to find a different font online. Use Google Fonts, MyFonts.com, 1001freefonts.com or a similar site to find an alphabet you like and print out the letters you need in a couple of different sizes (similar to those above, which are close to 36 and 28-point fonts). Remember that any fonts that aren't monoline (meaning they have some thick and some thin strokes rather than one consistent line weight) will be harder to trace and impossible to reproduce exactly without use of a calligraphy pen.

Step Three: Scale, Flourishing, and Personal Touches

We introduced each of these concepts in the Design Fundamentals and Technical Execution section. We will now look at each one more closely and explore specific options for making use of them in your signature. Read through the descriptions and consider what interests you in each one; as always, it's a good idea to make notes about your ideas. Later, we'll do a design exercise where you will experiment with how to incorporate these elements into your signature.

SCALE

Manipulating scale is one of the easiest ways to transform your signature, as changes in scale alone (even with few letter modifications) can have a significant impact on the look and feel of your writing.

We want to think about scale in two separate, but related places:

1. Scale of capitals to minuscules.
2. Scale of x-height to ascenders/descenders on lowercase letters.

These scales may or may not be the same. (In other words, the height of your ascenders and descenders on your minuscules may be equal to the height of your capitals, or it may be different.)

Playing with the scale of your capitals usually means playing with the entire size of the letter (height and width). By contrast, when we think about scale for your lowercase letters, we want to experiment *mainly* with changing the height of the ascenders and descenders, while holding the x-height and width of the letter constant.

I recommend experimenting with exaggerated scales on your capitals and minuscules.

Capitals can easily be five times (or more) the height of your minuscule x-height (indeed, some of the sample signatures we've looked at have capitals that are more than ten times the height of the x-height), but they typically will *not* be too much taller than your tallest ascender. Many of the signatures I love are eye-catching mainly because of their capitals. In addition to design impact, large capitals confer another distinct advantage: the more pronounced the capital, the easier it is to get away with more relaxed – even abstract – lowercase letters. The eye is drawn to the capitals, and the overall mark looks pleasing even when the minuscules lose some legibility.

Dramatic minuscule scale is another common quality of exciting signatures. Tall, eye-catching ascenders and long, striking descenders add interest and create a lot of opportunity for playing with embellishments, contrast, and the overall balance of your signature design.

Let's look at some examples of how altering the scales of capitals and minuscules changes the look and feel of a signature.

Minuscule Scale of Three
with Large Capitals

Minuscule Scale of Four
with Small Capitals

The first signature has a relatively common scale setup. Both the capitals and the minuscules have a dramatic scale, and the signature feels well-balanced and looks attractive.

In the second signature, there is an even more dramatic minuscule scale and capitals that are slightly smaller than the tallest ascenders. This is something you'll almost never see. Even though this signature is well-executed and still pretty, the sense of balance feels off. Look back between the first and second signature and see if you have an instinctive reaction to which one feels more "right."

In each of the next three samples, the height of the capitals is equal to the height of the ascenders. The minuscule scales become increasingly dramatic.

Consider how the look of the signature changes as the scale increases. Additionally, what can you notice about the third sample?

Oftentimes, when you switch to using such a striking minuscule scale, you will need to make changes to some of the letterforms in order to maintain visual balance. In the name Farrah Ellington, there are four letters in a row – right in the middle of the name ("h," "E," "ll") – which reach the maximum height of the ascender line. This concentration of tall letters begins to impact

Miniscule Scale of Two   Miniscule Scale of Three   Miniscule Scale of Four

the balance of the overall design as the minuscule scale increases. As a result, the loop of the second "l" has been shortened in the third sample to preserve visual balance.

There are many ways that balance could have been maintained (i.e. increasing the scale of the capitals to make the "E" stand out more than the "h" and "ll," lengthening the descender of the "g" and creating a more dramatic flourish, etc.), but this approach fits with the overall playful vibe/style of the signature and helps restore balance as well.

When writing minuscules, in addition to making ascenders and descenders taller or shorter (in relation to the x-height) you have the options of making loops fatter or thinner, maintaining perfect ovals or using less standard shapes, or adding loops in areas that would typically only be retraced (like on the ascender of a lowercase "t"). To achieve a polished design, you'll want to keep a few guidelines in mind:

1. Keep the x-height consistent throughout the letters in your name.
2. Don't mess with the width or shape of the letters too much between the baseline and the x-height.
3. The height and length of ascenders and descenders should be similar.

Let's look at a few more examples.

Farrah Ellington   *Farrah Ellington*   *Farrah Ellington*

Thin Loops   *Fat Loops*   *Irregular Loops*

Remember, letters produced by hand are – almost by definition – imperfect. These guidelines are meant to inform you about which specific characteristics contribute to a design that our eyes will interpret as professional, sophisticated, or beautiful. Heights, widths, and shapes don't have to be, and never will be, perfect. Strive for a sense of sameness and consistency in your hand but leave the rulers and protractors in the drawer. To explore these concepts even further, remember there are always more examples readily available on our Pinterest board at https://www.pinterest.com/createasignature.

FLOURISHING

There are a couple of simple rules to stick to when it comes to adding flourishes to your signature:

1. Keep them to a minimum and avoid crossing too many lines over each other.
2. They usually look best either at the beginning or end of a word, or on letters with ascenders and descenders.
3. Think about how any flourish you add will impact the visual balance of your signature.

Let's face it, flourishing can be fun. It's perfectly okay, and even advisable, to experiment with all different types of flourishes during your practice. But when it comes to locking down your final signature, resist the temptation to overdo it. **I suggest adding in only one to two flourishes.** More than that begins to look silly, cluttered, and cashiers will look at you funny if you have to stand there holding up the line for a full minute signing your receipt.

You've already got statement capitals, masterful minuscules, and intelligent use of scale at your disposal – and, before you begin your exercises, I will teach you a simple trick that will help you learn to write at any slant you want. We want to think about flourishing as the finishing touch on your design and wield it with restraint.

Consider adding flourishes in the following ways:

1. Use an underline
2. Use an overline
3. Extend one or two exit strokes
4. Create unexpected relationships between letters (overlapping letters, use an exit stroke to cross a t, etc.)

One of the most common and pleasing flourishes is the underline. An underline can span the full length of your signature, or only a part of it (for example, from the second letter on, or under lowercase letters only). It can also be its own distinct element, or it can be attached to one of the letters of your name. This is often done by extending the exit stroke (the last stroke of a letter) from the first or last letter in your name into an underline. It can be a straight, single line, or a looped, fancy one that doubles back over itself several times. You could even have two underlines – one extending from the exit stroke of your first capital and stretching beneath your first name, and another extending from the exit stoke of your second capital, stretching beneath your last name.

Another fun way to flourish is to add a simple "overline." These are straight lines or arcs going over the top of a signature. They are almost always attached to the first or last letter, or the ascender of a lowercase letter – especially "t." If kept simple and done well, these can sometimes even be used in addition to an underline, creating a nice counterbalance.

These signatures showcase just a few ways to utilize full or partial underlines or overlines (or both) effectively.

Dannie Valenti

Jhon Sargent

M. Michael

As with all flourishes, be cognizant about how many other letters/lines you're crossing through, and where. Overlapping too much or too carelessly often ends up looking messy and can even seem like you're crossing out your name.

The next option is to exaggerate the exit stroke of one or two letters. This is a similar concept to making connected underlines or overlines; you'll still typically be taking advantage of first/last letters or ascenders/descenders to do it, you'll just be extending them into a different shape. This is often done with the final letter in a signature – as we saw in many of the samples in the Design Fundamentals and Technical execution section.

The exit stroke of the letter can be extended down, up, or even straight out to the side to excellent effect. These extensions are opportunities for "true" flourishes – you can choose to loop the extended line and trail it down, up, or sideways as much as you like. Sometimes, a nice effect is achieved by having a flourish turn back toward its point of origin.

Try to maintain a cohesive shape in your flourishes – a sense of an oval if your letters are round and flowing, or a straight line if your letters are sharper or more angular. Consider the differences between these samples:

Theodora Ravenett

Margaret Ava

If you pursue more advanced or artistic writing forms, like calligraphy, hand lettering, or penmanship, you'll find that there are an almost infinite number of ways to flourish. Most of them, however, are simply extensions or exaggerated versions of the examples above.

Additional flourishes are rare outside of ornamental penmanship - loops upon loops, which extend into whimsical drawings of flowers or birds, while beautiful, are hardly practical features of a modern signature.

You can also use your extended strokes to create interesting relationships between letters. Remember the way the loop of the first capital "P" in the "Phillip Pratt" signature in the Design Fundamentals and Technical Execution section was extended to act as the loop of the other two "p's?" Or how the top line of the "T" extended to form the crossbar of the "A" in "Alex Tuffy?"

This device is used all the time in signatures and can add interest while preventing a signature from looking cluttered, since the one extended stroke often takes the place of other lines that would be there. In the example below, the crossbar of the "t" acts as the join between the "t" and the "h" – and the extended "B" helps to form the "x." The signature retains a clean, tidy look even with these "overlapping letters."

Ruth Baxter

Consider "stacking" your signature (have your first name sitting partly or fully on top of your last name) rather than having your names next to each other in a line – this opens up lots of additional opportunities for making letters interact.

CONNECTING STROKES AND ALTERNATE LETTERFORMS
Another way that signatures convey a sense of personality is through their connecting strokes, or the way the letters are joined together.

Established scripts like The Palmer Method (the cursive alphabet most kids learn in school in the U.S.), Copperplate, and Spencerian all have set model alphabets where every letter joins to every other letter in a prescribed way. These letters and joins, are studied, practiced, and executed according to the "rules" set by the creators of each respective hand.

In daily handwriting, however, joins often occur as an organic evolution of our natural writing. This means that they are a distinguishing factor in what makes our writing uniquely ours.

If you came of age after the era of personal computers began, it's likely that cursive was not emphasized as part of your education. In my case, for example, I learned cursive in third grade, then almost never used it again for anything – other than my signature. As a result, my signature employed the joins prescribed by the model cursive alphabet that I was taught. Print writing, by definition, has no joins, but as we get older and need greater speed in our print writing, we often begin to spontaneously connect some of our letters. This results in a sort of print-script hybrid that is particular to us. So, somewhat ironically, your print writing may be the place to look for inspiration on how to join up the letters in your signature.

If you're going to replace the more "standard" joins with something else, the best policy is to use the joins that are native to your writing – as this will be the easiest and most authentic approach. After all, your signature is a representation of you – so you don't need to go looking for alternative ways of joining up unless you're trying to solve a specific problem.

Feel free to adapt joins from your print writing for use in your cursive signature – this can have a great simplifying effect in addition to adding character to your design. Moving away from the frilly formality of cursive toward more functional "print joins" often makes signing faster and easier.

Furthermore, there is no rule that says all the letters in your signature must be joined to each other. Feel free to get creative with your joins, or to choose not to join at all at strategic points.

You may have two (or more) letters next to each other in your name which create a difficult or awkward join. For example, the letter "o" is typically joined to the letter following it via a connecting stroke from the top of the "o" – this can be challenging when the following letter, like "s" or "r," can only be formed correctly by beginning at the baseline. Sometimes, swapping in a print-style "s" or "r," or eliminating the join between these letters, can solve the problem.

Consider these examples, which use limited joins and mostly print-style letters but are still instantly recognizable as signatures.

Thomas Herzberg

Thomas Herzberg

Gerald Taylor

Gerald Taylor

If your name is long, you may need a brief pause at some point in the middle of your name to ensure that you write the last letters as well as you write the first letters. There may be a natural place to eliminate a join, which creates an opportunity for a planned pen lift, allowing you to write the remainder of your name more comfortably.

If you need to lift your pen in the middle of your name, but want to join all the letters, you can do so. It's common for people to need to lift their pens every four to five letters to maintain neatness and consistency in their writing. My maiden name was nine letters long, and my signature would have been greatly improved if I had paused halfway through. If you realize that your hand starts to fatigue after a certain letter in your name, just lift your pen, slide your hand along the line, then touch back down on top of your last stroke and continue writing where you left off. Your writing will benefit, and no one will ever know but you.

If you choose not to join all the letters within your name(s), pay special attention to your spacing. It's easy to place two letters too far apart when they have no connecting stroke between them, resulting in a large negative space (blank area) within your name, which causes the eye to stumble over the area.

All this being said, bear in mind that the less times you lift your pen from the paper, the faster you'll be able to sign. Use pen lifts where you need them, but be economical about your choices.

Your Practice Program

Time to get started on mastering your new signature!

Here's how we'll do it:

- Phase One: you'll use your chosen statement capitals and the minuscule practice alphabet to improve your fine motor skills and achieve the quality of strokes and level of consistency of letter size, shape, spacing, and slant that lays the foundation for a great signature. You'll start by tracing the model letters, and then continue on with freehand practice until you're comfortable.
- Phase Two: you'll use your improved writing skills to do a design experiment – testing out different scales, flourishes, and personal touches.
- Phase Three: you'll practice integrating your chosen embellishments into your signature.

Remember: each *practice session* should take approximately 30 minutes, including ten minutes for state exercises, writing warmups, and analytical practice, and the remaining 20 minutes for physical writing practice. Each *physical writing exercise* may take longer or shorter than 20 minutes, depending on your comfort level with the material. If you experience no pain or discomfort, you can write for longer stretches or do multiple sessions in a day, if desired. For most people, however, 30 minutes works well.

You should do each exercise as many times as it takes for you to get relatively comfortable with it – not until you're producing "perfect" letters. The exercises in this program build on each other incrementally. The amount of time it takes to master a given letter or shape will vary for everyone, depending largely on your experience and skill level at the start. This is another reason why your analytical practice is so important; it's the way you'll decide if you need to linger longer on a given exercise, or if there are some you can skip altogether.

Your Secret Weapon: Slant Guidelines

Since we all write our letters with varying degrees of slant (they can lean left, upright, or to the right), and since we may even want to change the slant of our signatures, we need a flexible and customizable way to help us maintain our chosen slant.

Calligraphers, who work with many different alphabets with a variety of slants, often do this by drawing in their own horizontal and angled lines. This allows them to customize the angle/degree of their guidelines to fit the slant of the alphabet they are working with exactly. This, however, is too time-consuming and cumbersome for our purposes – so we will take a different approach.

On page 118 you'll find two sets of Slant Guidelines – a Wide set and a Narrow set. You can tear or cut these out of your book for use with tracing exercises, but don't write directly on them – you will want to reuse them. Many of your exercises will ask you to place either the Wide or Narrow guidelines underneath your workbook paper, in order to create custom guidelines for any slant with almost no effort.

Here's how it works:
1. Tear or cut your Wide or Narrow Slant Guidelines (as specified in your exercise) out of your book.
2. Place the guidelines on the table with the lines running vertically (perpendicular to the edge of the table). Remember to place the paper slightly off to your right if you're right-handed, and slightly to your left if you're left-handed.
3. Get a piece of tracing paper (or any paper with enough translucency to allow the guidelines to show through), and place it on top of your slant guidelines with the lines running horizontally.

That's it! Now you can instantly create perfect guidelines for any slant by simply rotating your top sheet clockwise or counterclockwise, as shown on the next page. The slant guideline sheet should never move[05].

05
___
Pro Tips

Always keep a few extra sheets of paper underneath the guidelines for a softer writing surface.

I like to tape my slant guidelines to the table to prevent any sliding around while I'm writing. I use a low-tack artist's tape, which is easy to remove from the paper and the table. Always remove tape from your guidelines paper carefully, and use your discretion if you choose to apply tape directly to your table.

transparent workbook paper
slant guideline page

rotate counterclockwise
for a steeper slant

You may need to shift the tracing paper around on top of the slant guidelines several times in the course of writing practice in order to fill all the worksheet lines fully.

I first learned of this ingenious trick in a conversation with penmanship expert Marcus Carlini. In addition to being incredibly easy, it's based on fundamentally sound principles for mastering consistent slant. In a paper for IAMPETH (International Association of Master Penman, Engrossers, and Teachers of Handwriting) Carlini explains, "...slant lines should point directly towards you. When you are pulling downstrokes, they go towards your body. It is much easier to maintain a slant when all of your downstrokes appear vertical. This is the same for every script. If I want to write at a 45-degree angle for a heavily slanted Ornamental Script, I merely rotate my page more. If I'm writing Italic with a broad nib, I rotate my page less. Downstrokes are always towards your body."

Slant Guidelines Instruction

Phase One Exercises

This phase is comprised of a string of exercises in which you practice writing each letter of your name individually, and then in sequence with the letters preceding it, until you can move smoothly from the first letter in your name to the last. Your goal in your initial exercises is to approximate the model letters and thereby improve the rhythm and discipline of your writing. Personal modifications come in the Phase Two and Three exercises.

This means that, if you are already comfortable with your handwriting/cursive in general, you may want to skip or shorten many of the exercises in this Phase. I recommend – at the very least – reading through the summary below, the Detailed Instructions for Exercise #1, and the Aided Review for Exercise #1. But it's best if you give each exercise a try, and simply shorten it according to your needs (for example, you may find that you only need a few lines of practice for each letter). You will also find all of your state management exercise instructions at the start of each of the Phase One exercises.

If your handwriting is not as fluid or shapely as you want it to be, this phase is invaluable.

Before you read the detailed instructions for your first exercise, let's look at the exercise flow for my name (Brooke Vega) as an example. Remember, each exercise does **not** represent a 30-minute practice session. You might only need a single line of practice on a letter before you can reproduce it relatively reliably, or you may need to practice 10 pages or more before you're satisfied with your results. It all depends on your starting point and the standards you set for yourself.

You can also choose to trace a few lines of each new letter, before starting your freehand practice.

Exercises for learning to sign "Brooke Vega":
1. Practice capital "B" on its own.
2. Practice "r" on its own.

3. Practice "Br" all together.
4. Practice "o" on its own.
5. Practice "Bro" all together.
6. Practice "Broo" all together (in this case, I didn't need to practice "o" again on its own, since I had just done that a couple of exercises prior).
7. Practice "k" on its own.
8. Practice "Brook" all together.
9. Practice "e" on its own.
10. Practice "Brooke" all together.

Next, I repeated the process for my last name (Vega), and then practiced writing "Brooke Vega" all together.

Make sure to use the Phase One Workbook Paper for these exercises. It is designed specifically to help you master a consistent x-height and is set to the scale of your practice alphabet. [Note: If you use the larger of the two practice alphabet sizes, the x-height of your minuscules will bump up against the x-height guideline. If you use the smaller of the two sizes, the x-height of your minuscules will fall just short of the x-height guideline. Pay attention to how the traced letters sit on the guidelines and reproduce them accordingly.]

Exercise #1 – Detailed Instructions

Set up your writing space as best you can to approximate the setup described in the Setup and Tools section. Try to maintain good posture throughout the exercise, but use your normal grip unless you've determined that you need to make changes.

This exercise involves both tracing and freehand practice. Whenever you begin tracing or writing a new letter, take a moment to think about the most efficient way to move through the strokes required to create the letter. When in doubt about where to start and finish the letter, keep this perfect, concise guideline in mind, "Order of strokes usually flows naturally from left to right, top to bottom, with minimum backtracking" (Sheila Waters, *Foundations of Calligraphy*). Make this your mantra, and repeat it whenever writing a letter for the first time.

EXERCISE GOAL
Increase your level of comfort with writing your first statement capital.

STATE MANAGEMENT EXERCISE

The Joy of Loving Kindness adapted from Chade-Meng Tan's contribution to *Tools of Titans*, by Tim Ferriss.

If you're in a public place, identify two strangers and think to yourself "I wish for this person to be happy, and I wish for that person to be happy." Don't just think the words by rote – really let yourself feel it. You can do this with your eyes open or closed, just remember not to stare like a crazy person.

If you're not in public, bring two people to mind (these should be friends or family – people you love or feel warmly toward) and wish for each one to be happy. Repeat this process as many times as you like, until you feel happy and relaxed. In Tan's words "This is the joy of loving-kindness. It turns out that being on the giving end of a kind thought is rewarding in and of itself.... All other things being equal, to increase your happiness, all you have to do is randomly wish for somebody else to be happy. That is all. It basically takes no time and effort."

PHYSICAL WRITING PRACTICE

1. Tear or cut the page with your first statement capital out of your book. If you are not using tracing paper, skip to step three of this exercise, and utilize the Phase One worksheet paper provided on page 122. If you are using tracing paper, print out several pages of the Phase One worksheet paper you obtained from signing up for the newsletter on the companion website at createasignature.com. Put your tracing paper worksheet on top of your statement capital page, placing the first blank line underneath the letter, as shown on the next page. Trace over it. Move the paper slightly to the left, and trace again. Continue doing this until you've traced one or two full lines of your capital. Keep your awareness on the feel of the movement.

2. Set aside your statement capital page. Tear or cut your Wide Slant Guidelines page out of your book and place it on the table, with the lines straight up and down, perpendicular to the edge of the table. Place your workbook paper from the previous step on top of your slant guidelines. Rotate the top page to align the downstrokes of your traced letters with the slant guidelines.

3. Practice your statement capital freehand, continuously using your model statement capital as a reference. Do not add in any additional flourishes at this stage, and don't worry if the slant of your model capital letter isn't the

06

———

See the section above (How to Use Slant Guidelines) for a review of the detailed instructions on setup.

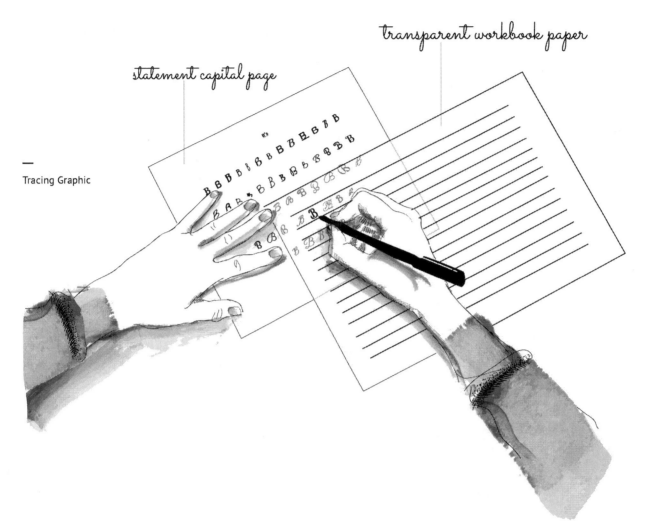

statement capital page

transparent workbook paper

Tracing Graphic

slant you ultimately want in your signature (we'll fix that later). Fill all the remaining lines on your workbook page with freehand practice of this letter, and use additional workbook pages to continue the exercise according to your needs and your level of comfort.

ANALYTICAL PRACTICE
(To be done immediately following this practice session, or immediately preceding the next session)

Great job! You just:
- Set and achieved a specific, attainable goal
- Learned a state management exercise
- Learned to use your slant guidelines
- Made progress toward strengthening your fine motor skills

Make sure to recognize these successes and reward yourself.

Now, spend a few minutes reviewing your freehand practice. You'll need to critique it in order to set a new goal for your next session. Handle this just like we did in the Self-Assessment section: avoid general value statements about your writing (like "it's good" or "it's bad"). Instead, ask yourself, "How are the letters I wrote different from or similar to the model letter?" Be specific, and try to note at least two positives, as well a couple of areas for improvement.

Your analysis might look something like this:
- Positives:
  - Consistent letter size (width and height)
  - Consistent slant
- Needs improvement:
  - Movement felt unfamiliar and I had to write slowly; I need to work on fluidity/confidence of my motion.
  - [Loop/exit stroke/etc.] on my letters did not match the model letter; I need to work on making it [fatter/thinner/bigger/smaller/curvier/straighter/etc.].

Your notes could also be related to your grip, posture, or state. Did you notice yourself clutching the pen tightly? Slumping your shoulders? Holding your breath? Being hard on yourself about your writing? It's a great idea to capture these observations and make improving your ability to remain relaxed and enjoy your writing time an explicit part of your goals.

After you finish making your notes, choose one or two points from your "Needs improvement" list, and make these your goals for your next practice session. Make sure they are specific, attainable, and measurable. After you set the goal, you should be able to answer the question, "How will I know if I've been successful at moving toward this goal after my practice session?" If you can't answer that, break your goal down into more specific and realistic components.

Exercise #1 – Aided Review
How did you feel doing this exercise?

If it felt too hard, let's make it easier. If it felt too easy, let's make it harder.

07
___

These strategies can be applied to any exercise in this book, not just exercise #1.

08

——

Adapted from *Spencerian Key to Practical Penmanship*, compiled by H.C. Spencer from the works of Platt R. Spencer.

Strategies [07] for lowering the danger level:

1. If your trouble stemmed from the "Beautiful Workbook Complex" and you found yourself slipping into perfectionism, consider rereading that section and adding in warmup writing exercises like those on the next page [08]. Warmup exercises are a great way to get pen to paper and start marking up your workbook. Your goal while doing them should be to get your body relaxed and to work toward a smooth, light movement of your hand. You don't need to, and shouldn't, care about reproducing the warmup shapes exactly as shown.

2. If your first capital is elaborate and you're having trouble executing the whole thing in one go, consider breaking it down into two or three smaller components and practicing each one individually before putting it all back together. You can always do this with any letter you're struggling with, and even though it seems like it's adding to the amount of practice you're doing, it often leads you to master your "trouble letters" more quickly. I used this technique with both the lowercase "k" and "g" in my name, as I was struggling to produce the size and shape of the ascender and descender I wanted on them. So, I practiced several pages of just the ascender and descender, then returned to practicing each letter as a whole.

3. Try writing your letter in a very large size on a dry erase board (or a mirror), chalk board, or even a cheap poster board or large piece of newsprint paper taped to a wall (make sure the ink you're using won't bleed through onto your wall). Sometimes, writing a tough letter at a large size makes it easier to spot where you're going wrong and fix the issue. Plus, writing on a vertical or angled surface (especially a dry erase board, where the marker glides over the surface with almost no friction) makes fluid motion easier to achieve than when writing on a horizontal surface where you have to support some of your weight with your writing arm.

4. Just repeat Exercise #1 until you're comfortable moving on! The exercises are broken down according to what sequence of material is most advantageous for you to practice – there is no implication that each exercise should only take you one try.

Strategies for increasing the challenge:

1. Try altering your model letters to sit at the slant you want while you're practicing them freehand. Not sure which slant you want your final signature to have yet? Experiment. Take your first capital and write a line of it with a

backwards slant, a line with it upright (no slant), and another line or two with slight or deep forward slants. Remember, just rotate your workbook paper on top of your slant guidelines to create the guidelines you need.

2. Consider eliminating the tracing step altogether prior to practicing your model letters freehand.

3. Move quickly through the Phase One exercises, or, if you're feeling really confident, skip straight ahead to the Phase Two design experiment.

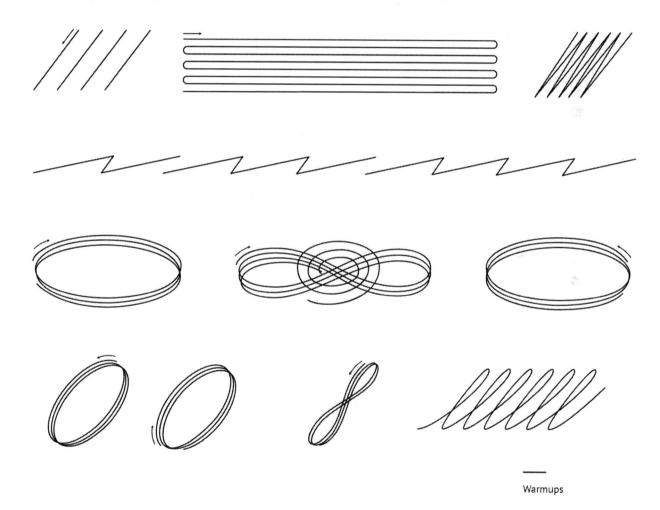

Warmups

Exercise #2 – Detailed Instructions

Review the goal you set at the end of your last practice session (or complete your analytical practice now, if you haven't yet), so it's fresh in your mind as you begin your next exercise.

STATE MANAGEMENT EXERCISE

Manipulate your mind with music! Put on a song you love – preferably something that makes you feel focused, excited, creative, hopeful, or calm. We often create very strong associations between certain music and specific memories/emotions. Because of this, we can use music to intentionally trigger positive physiological states when we need them. When you start your song, lean into it – sing along, dance or otherwise move your body to encourage those positive associations to take root. For extra credit, make a writing practice playlist that you can play throughout your sessions (or find a premade one on Spotify, Pandora, or whichever music application you love best).

09

You have two different sizes of letters to choose from. Begin working with the size that mostly closely resembles your natural handwriting - or (if different) the size that closest to how large or small you want the letters in your final signature to be.

If you are on the fence about which size to choose, or if you have a lot of difficulty during the exercise, consider using the larger of the two sizes. It is often easier to correctly perceive the shapes of each letter, and to spot differences between your work and the model letter, when the size is larger.

PHYSICAL WRITING PRACTICE

1. Tear or cut the page with your Minuscule Practice Alphabet [09] out of your book. If you're not using tracing paper, turn to a blank Phase One workbook page and skip to step three of this exercise. Otherwise, put one of your tracing paper worksheets on top of your minuscule alphabet page, placing the first blank line underneath the model letter of the second letter in your name. Trace over it. Move paper slightly to the left, and trace again. Continue doing this until you've traced one or two full lines. Keep your awareness on the feel of the movement.

2. Set aside your Minuscule Practice Alphabet. Tear or cut your **Narrow** Slant Guidelines paper out of your book and place it on the table, with the lines straight up and down, perpendicular to the edge of the table. Place your workbook paper from the previous step on top of your slant guidelines. Rotate the top page to align the downstrokes of your traced letters with the slant guidelines.

3. Fill your workbook page with freehand practice of the second letter in your name, using your minuscule alphabet as a reference. Keep moving and don't expect perfection, but maintain awareness of how your letter formation is similar or different to the model letter.

ANALYTICAL PRACTICE

Do your self-critique and make notes about the positives and areas requiring improvement from this exercise. Remember to reward yourself for spending the time and effort to get your practice done.

Exercise #3 – Detailed Instructions

Review the goal you set at the end of your last practice session, or set your goal(s) now if you haven't.

STATE MANAGEMENT EXERCISE

Box Breathing/Four-Square Breathing

This breathing exercise has been lauded by a wide variety of academics and practitioners, from researchers, to police units and Navy Seals, to yogis. It produces a calming effect that can be felt almost immediately, and is proven to significantly reduce stress and anxiety, and to otherwise help regulate your autonomic nervous system.

Note: *especially if you're new to breathing exercises, pay close attention to how you feel as you move through this exercise. If you begin to feel dizzy or faint at any time, resume normal breathing until the feeling passes.*

1. Make sure you're sitting comfortably.
2. Exhale all the air from your lungs, knowing that the more old, stale air you release, the more fresh, energizing oxygen you can breathe in.
3. Breathe in through your nose, timing your breath so that your lungs are full at a count of four. (To ensure that you are creating deep, diaphragmatic breaths, it can be helpful to place one hand on your chest and one hand on your belly. If you are breathing diaphragmatically, your stomach will expand more than your chest.)
4. Hold your breath through a count of four.
5. Exhale to a count of four.
6. Repeat three to four times. As you become used to the exercise, you can continue it for slightly longer periods (five to ten minutes).

As you gain comfort with this exercise, practice "following" your breath through your body. What can you notice as you inhale through your nose? The cool freshness of the air? The opening expansiveness of your body? What can you notice as you exhale? The relaxing, sinking feeling of your body as it lets go? The warm, soft quality of the air you exhale?

The more present and engaged you can be with your breath in this exercise, the greater the impact. You don't have to *think* about the feelings; just observe and enjoy them.

PHYSICAL WRITING PRACTICE

Practice writing the first and second letters of your name together, freehand. If needed, trace a couple of lines of each letter first, to remind your hand of the correct movements.

If you have tracing paper, you can also use your Narrow slant guidelines to aid you in your freehand practice. At this point, don't worry if the slant of your capital and the slant of your first minuscule are different – just strive for consistency in each letter.

If you're feeling good and want a little more of a challenge, try to write both letters at the same slant.

ANALYTICAL PRACTICE

You know the drill – do it!

Phase One Midpoint – Aided Review

> ❝ *I have this idea that art should be difficult... and we think it shouldn't be, and this is the problem, in my opinion, with people who want to become artists.... This starts when we're very, very young. We try to make something, we don't have a very long attention span, we give up.* ❞
> *Nobody tells us that it's supposed to be hard. And then that's it.*
>
> – Brooke Shaden, *Fine Art Photography: The Complete Guide*

> ❝ *You know the great thing, though, is that change can be so constant that you don't even feel the difference until there is one. It can be so slow that you don't know that your life is better or worse, until it is. Or it can just blow you away, make you something different in an instant.* ❞
>
> – *Life as a House*

Take a moment to assess your progress so far. You're three exercises in, and perhaps have done two or three times that many practice sessions. If practice so far has been a joy, and you feel like you're improving at a satisfactory rate, you can skip this section and just keep trucking. If it's been tough at all (whether to be consistent, or get the results you want), consider the following:

How have you felt about practice? Has it been fun? Has it been work? Do you feel like you're making progress, or like you're just proving over and over that you can't write the way you want to?

Often, all that separates "talented" people from "regular" people is that "talented" people keep trying, even when no progress seems to be happening. The implication here is that all you have to do to be exceptional is to keep going when most people would have quit (and most people quit at the beginning).

What do you think is holding you back?

1. Technical deficiency
   a. If you truly think that lack of ability is holding you back from making progress, you simply need more practice. If you need a little inspiration, search online for the Gatorade commercial "The Secret to Victory." (In case you're curious, I have no affiliation with Gatorade – it's just an amazing video!)
2. Inner critic
   a. If you find yourself struggling against your inner critic, try writing in the dark. Set up your practice space and then turn out the lights – leaving only one or two dim sources on (a candle, a night light, a closet light, etc.). You should be able to see your hands and the paper in front of you, but it should be hard to make out your writing. Do your practice per usual and allow the limited visual stimuli to help you focus more completely on the feel of writing. Do this exercise as often as needed.
3. Criteria for success is too high
   a. The reason we set only one or two specific goals for any practice session and constantly ask ourselves "How will I know if I've been successful in this session?" is that this method of goal setting aligns with the reality of how we learn. Karen Pryor, an expert in behavioral psychology and positive reinforcement training with decades of experience working with animals and people, unpacks this concept well in her book *Don't Shoot the Dog!*:
   "Take learning to putt. Putting a golf ball depends on sending it the right distance – not short of the cup and not past it or over it – and sending it the right direction, not to one side of the cup or the other. If I were going to teach myself to putt, I would practice these separately.... Often when we seem to show no progress in a skill, no matter how much we practice, it is because

we are trying to improve two or more things at once. Practice is not shaping. Repetition, by itself, may ingrain mistakes just as easily as improvements. One needs to think: Does this behavior have more than one attribute? Is there some way to break it down and work on different criteria separately? When you address both of these questions, many problems solve themselves."

It's important to note that this does not mean that you must focus on only one skill at a time until you master it. If you focus only on letter sizing, for example, in every single practice session until you have "perfectly" sized letters, you may grow bored. You can alternate between goals within the same session – just focus your attention on only one at a time.

Let's say you begin a practice session with two goals: improve consistency of letter size and increase fluidity of movement. Choose just one to start with. If, after three lines of practice, you notice an improvement in your letter size – perhaps you write several letters in a row all the same size – let yourself end on a good note for that goal, and switch to focusing on fluidity of movement.

If you're struggling for any reason, the most important thing is to just keep trying. Try out the different techniques in this book and notice what is working for you and what isn't. Adjust your approach accordingly.

Exercise #4 – Detailed Guidelines
Review the goal you set at the end of your last practice session or set your goal now if you haven't.

STATE MANAGEMENT EXERCISE
Pure Contour Drawing – adapted from *Drawing on the Right Side of the Brain* by Betty Edwards
This exercise is somewhat different from your other state management exercises. Rather than focusing on bringing your physiological state to a place of relaxed focus so that you can optimize your performance during practice, the goal here is to engage your brain's visual mode (the right side of your brain) while simultaneously quieting the analytical (left side) of your brain.

It is also an excellent way to challenge and improve your visual-motor integration, as you work to correctly perceive and then reproduce abstract shapes.

Follow the steps below.

1. Take out a pencil and a piece of scrap paper.
2. Stabilize the paper on the table with a couple of paperweights or with tape.
3. Set a timer for five minutes.
4. Take a pencil in your drawing hand and place it in the middle of the paper, ready to draw. Now, turn away from the paper and your drawing hand and focus, instead, on the palm of your non-dominant hand. Fix your attention on one wrinkle in your palm.
5. Without looking at your paper, draw that wrinkle. Then begin drawing all the wrinkles near it or branching off from it, focusing on the center of your palm. Don't draw the outline of your hand or try to convey the overall shape of your palm in any way – draw only the lines of the wrinkles.
6. Draw until the timer goes off.

Betty Edwards explains, "Pure Contour drawing is the most efficient way I know to prepare the brain for visual tasks. The verbal brain mode, which is seemingly easily bored, finds the task so tedious (and so 'useless' in terms of producing a recognizable, nameable image) that it quickly drops out, enabling the visual mode to come forward. R-mode [the right side of the brain], however, seems to find detailed complexity fascinating and will keep on with the drawing until the timer sounds. If, at some point in your Pure Contour drawing, you found yourself becoming *interested* in your perception of the tiny area in your palm, that indicates a shift to the visual mode. If not, try another short session."

PHYSICAL WRITING PRACTICE
Repeat the steps from Exercise #2 with the third letter in your name; first tracing it using the Minuscule Practice Alphabet, then practicing it freehand, with the help of your Narrow Slant Guidelines if desired.

Don't forget to do your **analytical practice!**

Exercise #5 – Detailed Guidelines
Review the goal you set at the end of your last practice session or set your goal(s) now if you haven't.

STATE MANAGEMENT EXERCISE

Practicing Gratitude with Tony Robbins and Tim Ferriss

This is my all-time favorite exercise. I do it on a regular basis and have recommended it to dozens of friends and family members. The exercise is audio-based, so you'll need an internet connection to access it. At the time of writing, the direct link was https://tim.blog/2016/09/18/how-to-resolve-internal-conflict/ - but if you have trouble reaching the page, simply search for *Episode #186: Tony Robbins on How to Resolve Internal Conflict* on the podcast The Tim Ferriss Show.

The exercise begins at 2:40 on the audio file.

Enjoy!

PHYSICAL WRITING PRACTICE

Practice the first three letters of your name all together, tracing first to warm up if needed.

Use your Narrow Slant Guidelines to aid your freehand practice if desired.

As always, remember to do your analytical practice!

Exercises #6, #7, #8... #∞ - Detailed Guidelines

STATE MANAGEMENT EXERCISES

Try out a guided meditation app, like Headspace or Calm. Headspace is my personal favorite, and they offer a 10-day set of 10-minute meditations for free.

You can also repeat any of the state management exercises in this book at any time; the results will improve and intensify the more often each exercise is repeated.

PHYSICAL WRITING PRACTICE

The number of exercises you do in Phase One of the practice program is determined by how many letters are in your name. Continue practicing each letter of your name individually, and then in sequence with the letters preceding it, until you have completed all the letters in your name.

As you continue practicing, your comfort with producing letters freehand will increase – especially with the letters at the beginning of your name, as you'll be repeatedly rewriting them as you add each additional letter to your practice sequence. Allow yourself to settle into this comfort, and let your hand relax away from trying to perfectly reproduce the model letters, instead allowing the characteristics of your natural handwriting to creep back in. Continue to strive for consistency in your letterforms, but let the shape, size, slant, and even the joins of your letters begin to stray back toward your personal style.

An excellent way to encourage this process is to trace over a sample of your own writing that you like. When I was first trying to produce the "k" that I wanted for my own signature, perhaps one out of every 20 "k's" I wrote would turn out well. To help myself solidify the muscle memory of those well-executed and personally characteristic "k's," I would often place my tracing paper over them and trace over my own writing, rather than returning to the model letter. When it came time to work on the loop of my "g," I simply flipped my well-executed "k" upside down and traced the loop to prepare myself for making a "g" that felt balanced and uniform to the "k."

This type of tracing tends to feel more natural since you're following lines produced by your own movement, and the result is more unique to you than tracing a model letter. I learned this little hack from the book *Improve Your Handwriting* by Rosemary Sassoon and G SE Briem – a great resource if you want to improve your overall handwriting.

Phase Two – Design Exercise

Rough Signature Mockup

Now that you've gotten into the swing of practice and have started developing a disciplined hand, let's take a few minutes and experiment with design concepts for your new signature.

The goal of this exercise is to make a few simple mockups of what your final signature design might look like.

This will help you to think through whether you like how the capitals you chose look together or if you need to modify them, and to make some decisions about embellishments. Treat this as an experiment, and don't get too hung up on the details. Mockups, by definition, are imperfect; you're brainstorming here – you're not supposed to be able to execute your final design flawlessly at this point.

Make sure to use your Phase Two Workbook Paper for this exercise. It includes additional guidelines and space to help you experiment with scale and flourishes. Continue using the Phase Two Workbook Paper as long as needed (it's okay to keep using it even as you begin your Phase Three Exercises).

Instructions:
1. Look back at any notes you made about what design elements you liked in the Self-Assessment and Scale, Flourishing, and Personal Touches sections.
2. Write your signature on a blank workbook page (as you've been practicing it throughout Phase One of your exercises).
3. Look at the result and consider:
   a. What scale do you want to use for your capitals and your minuscules?
   b. Would you like to change the way you join any of the letters, or form them differently?
   c. What would happen if you tightened or widened the spacing between your letters?
   d. Where are there good opportunities to add flourishes – and how will you maintain visual balance? Do you want to add an underline?

    e. What repeating design elements could you use?

    f. How might you "break the rules" intelligently?

4. Re-write your name as many times as you like, experimenting with different scales and embellishments. Write slowly and visualize what your final design will look like. Focus on whether or not each experiment produces a version of your signature that has potential. You only need a few, rough mockups. But, if you desire, with a pencil, eraser, and a little patience, you can create a very nice approximation of your final signature, which you can then trace over for practice.

5. Decide which combination of elements you like best. Write down which mockup is your favorite, and why. This will be the signature you'll be working toward in the final phase.

Phase Three Exercises

Welcome to the final phase, and congrats on making it this far!

You're now a master of efficient practice, well-versed in self-critique, and equipped with a plethora of state management exercises and all the tools, tricks, and knowledge you need to make the most out of every exercise.

Similar to our practice approach in Phase One, you'll now practice your signature by adding one new element from your design mockup in each exercise and iterating until you have the result you want.

In general, I recommend beginning with elements that impact your whole signature (or a large portion of it), like slant, spacing, and scale. You may find that you need to make slight letter modifications as a result of these changes. If so, you can go back to practicing singular letters, then the full sequence as many times as needed.

Once you master the slant you want, begin practicing without using your slant guidelines – you don't want to become entirely dependent on them.

For the same reason, try to move from using the Phase Two Workbook paper to the Phase Three Workbook paper – which has far fewer guidelines – as soon as you are consistently writing to a scale you like.

From there, you can make any additional changes to letters, joins, and add in flourishes one at a time. Again, you can practice any modified letters in isolation, then add them back in to practice the full signature.

Throughout this phase of practice, move away from referring to your model letters and continue to let the characteristics of your natural handwriting return. Remember you can always trace over your particularly well-executed letters or signatures, and you can make similar use of your design mockup if you like it well enough.

Speed and Simplification

As you get nearer and nearer to mastering your desired signature, you may begin to wonder how to increase your signing speed – or you may even want to create a simplified version of your signature that is faster to write.

I highly recommend practicing on a dry erase board (or mirror). Write your signature on the dry erase board in varying sizes, as quickly as you can without compromising the correctness of your movements too much. Afterwards, practice your signature on paper again in the usual way. Many people see an immediate, dramatic difference, even after only 15-20 minutes of practice on the dry erase board. Repeat the exercise as often as needed.

You may find that practicing for speed in this way helps move you toward a slightly less legible, and therefore automatically simplified, signature. However, if you decide to actually alter your design to make it easier/quicker to sign, approach the process by considering where you can do one of two things:

1. Reduce the number of times you have to lift your pen while signing. Can you add a join or eliminate a complex flourish?
2. Simplify letters, making them easier to write less carefully and therefore more quickly. Review the signature samples in this book and look online to find ways that letters can be written more informally.

Generalizing the Skill

Once you're reliably producing the signature you want in your workbook, you'll want to start generalizing the skill, or solidifying your ability to make your mark reliably no matter what pen and paper you use, or what position you have to sign in.

Some generalization has been built into the practice you've already done – especially if you've tried the dry erase board exercises, or practiced writing in the dark. However, it's worth practicing explicitly, particularly if you plan to use your new signature on a daily basis or in a variety of situations.

To encourage generalization, practice with different pens on harder or softer surfaces, try signing while standing up, while curled up on the couch with a notebook in your lap, etc. Practice signing in different sizes, at different speeds, and with your eyes closed. If you have an opportunity to doodle – practice signing your name.

How Do You Know When You're Done?

   ——

66 *Every painting needs two artists, one to paint,
and one to tell him when to quit.* **99**

– Unknown

It's an age-old problem of artists – art can never be perfect, so how do you decide when to stop trying to improve a given project or design?

The only real litmus test for whether or not your signature is "done" is whether or not you like it. This is simple in theory, but it's sometimes tricky in practice. You've spent a significant amount of time designing, analyzing, and practicing your signature, part by part. Your mind is likely focused on the details, and it may cloud your judgment about the overall success of your redesign and practice.

If you're not sure whether or not you're done with your signature, the best advice is to get some distance from it – both literally and figuratively.

Artists often physically get up and step back from their projects in order to force a change of focus from the micro to the macro. Doing this will not only allow you to take in your overall design without getting caught up in the minutiae, but also to view it in a way much more similar to how other people will. No one else is going to look at your signature by putting it right under their nose and examining it letter by letter. They are much more likely to appreciate it from a somewhat greater distance, as a whole.

The other type of "distance" that can help is time. Stop practicing and thinking about your signature for a while. Give it a few days, or even a couple of weeks. You may be shocked at how differently you feel about it the next time you write it or see it.

Afterword

What You've Learned

Take some time to look back at your Self-Assessment – your first record of your starting signature inside this book – and appreciate how far you've come. Even your ability to compare your original signature and your new one in specific, meaningful terms is a testament to how much you've learned about design and the written arts.

But far beyond the design concepts you've learned or the disciplined hand you've cultivated is the approach to practice you've mastered and the art-confidence you've gained. The mindset you've exercised throughout this pursuit, and your increased understanding of behavioral psychology, neurobiology, and physiological state management will continue to serve you.

Only a few years ago, I was too insecure about my "innate" artistic endowments (or lack thereof) to even admit to friends and family that I wanted to try to succeed in any visual art form. I believed I had no artistic talent and that my desire to change that fact was laughable. I had a signature that embarrassed me every time I wrote it.

Since that time, I've experimented with oil painting, Chinese Brush Painting, charcoal and pencil drawing, penmanship, photography, and more. More importantly, I've tremendously enjoyed every one of these undertakings, and I look forward to many more years of practice and creation.

By creating a signature you love, you've proven to yourself – perhaps for the first time – that art is simply an interest pursued, and you have the capacity to do it well.

Go do anything you want now.

Yours in the art,

Brooke Vega

Slant Guidelines

DO NOT WRITE DIRECTLY ON THIS SHEET.

CREATE A SIGNATURE YOU LOVE • NARROW SLANT GUIDELINES

DO NOT WRITE DIRECTLY ON THIS SHEET.

119

DO NOT WRITE DIRECTLY ON THIS SHEET.

CREATE A SIGNATURE YOU LOVE • NARROW SLANT GUIDELINES

DO NOT WRITE DIRECTLY ON THIS SHEET.

Workbook
Phase One Workbook Paper

Write on top of the dotted line

Write down your observations and your one, specific goal for next session in the space below.

POSITIVES

NEEDS IMPROVEMENT

ONE, SPECIFIC THING I WILL WORK TO IMPROVE NEXT SESSION

CREATE A SIGNATURE YOU LOVE • PHASE ONE WORKBOOK PAPER

Write down your observations and your one, specific goal for next session in the space below.

| POSITIVES

| NEEDS IMPROVEMENT

| ONE, SPECIFIC THING I WILL WORK TO IMPROVE NEXT SESSION

Write down your observations and your one, specific goal for next session in the space below.

| POSITIVES

| NEEDS IMPROVEMENT

| ONE, SPECIFIC THING I WILL WORK TO IMPROVE NEXT SESSION

| ONE, SPECIFIC THING I WILL WORK TO IMPROVE NEXT SESSION

| NEEDS IMPROVEMENT

Write down your observations and your one, specific goal for next session in the space below.

| POSITIVES

Write down your observations and your one, specific goal for next session in the space below.

| POSITIVES

| NEEDS IMPROVEMENT

| ONE, SPECIFIC THING I WILL WORK TO IMPROVE NEXT SESSION

| CREATE A SIGNATURE YOU LOVE

Write down your observations and your one, specific goal for next session in the space below.

| POSITIVES

| NEEDS IMPROVEMENT

| ONE, SPECIFIC THING I WILL WORK TO IMPROVE NEXT SESSION

Write down your observations and your one, specific goal for next session in the space below.

| POSITIVES

| NEEDS IMPROVEMENT

| ONE, SPECIFIC THING I WILL WORK TO IMPROVE NEXT SESSION

✄

CREATE A SIGNATURE YOU LOVE • PHASE ONE WORKBOOK PAPER

Write down your observations and your one, specific goal for next session in the space below.

| POSITIVES

| NEEDS IMPROVEMENT

| ONE, SPECIFIC THING I WILL WORK TO IMPROVE NEXT SESSION

Write down your observations and your one, specific goal for next session in the space below.

| POSITIVES

| NEEDS IMPROVEMENT

| ONE, SPECIFIC THING I WILL WORK TO IMPROVE NEXT SESSION

| CREATE A SIGNATURE YOU LOVE • PHASE ONE WORKBOOK PAPER

Write down your observations and your one, specific goal for next session in the space below.

| POSITIVES

| NEEDS IMPROVEMENT

| ONE, SPECIFIC THING I WILL WORK TO IMPROVE NEXT SESSION

Write down your observations and your one, specific goal for next session in the space below.

| POSITIVES

| NEEDS IMPROVEMENT

| ONE, SPECIFIC THING I WILL WORK TO IMPROVE NEXT SESSION

✂
╎ **CREATE A SIGNATURE YOU LOVE** • PHASE ONE WORKBOOK PAPER

Write down your observations and your one, specific goal for next session in the space below.

╎ **POSITIVES**

╎ **NEEDS IMPROVEMENT**

╎ **ONE, SPECIFIC THING I WILL WORK TO IMPROVE NEXT SESSION**

Write down your observations and your one, specific goal for next session in the space below.

| POSITIVES

| NEEDS IMPROVEMENT

| ONE, SPECIFIC THING I WILL WORK TO IMPROVE NEXT SESSION

CREATE A SIGNATURE YOU LOVE • PHASE ONE WORKBOOK PAPER

Write down your observations and your one, specific goal for next session in the space below.

POSITIVES

NEEDS IMPROVEMENT

ONE, SPECIFIC THING I WILL WORK TO IMPROVE NEXT SESSION

| CREATE A SIGNATURE YOU LOVE • PHASE ONE WORKBOOK PAPER

Write down your observations and your one, specific goal for next session in the space below.

| POSITIVES

| NEEDS IMPROVEMENT

| ONE, SPECIFIC THING I WILL WORK TO IMPROVE NEXT SESSION

CREATE A SIGNATURE YOU LOVE • PHASE ONE WORKBOOK PAPER

Write down your observations and your one, specific goal for next session in the space below.

| POSITIVES

| NEEDS IMPROVEMENT

| ONE, SPECIFIC THING I WILL WORK TO IMPROVE NEXT SESSION

Phase Two Workbook Paper

Write down your observations and your one, specific goal for next session in the space below.

POSITIVES

NEEDS IMPROVEMENT

ONE, SPECIFIC THING I WILL WORK TO IMPROVE NEXT SESSION

✂

CREATE A SIGNATURE YOU LOVE • PHASE TWO WORKBOOK PAPER

Write down your observations and your one, specific goal for next session in the space below.

POSITIVES

NEEDS IMPROVEMENT

ONE, SPECIFIC THING I WILL WORK TO IMPROVE NEXT SESSION

Write down your observations and your one, specific goal for next session in the space below.

| POSITIVES

| NEEDS IMPROVEMENT

| ONE, SPECIFIC THING I WILL WORK TO IMPROVE NEXT SESSION

✂

CREATE A SIGNATURE YOU LOVE • PHASE TWO WORKBOOK PAPER

Write down your observations and your one, specific goal for next session in the space below.

| POSITIVES

| NEEDS IMPROVEMENT

| ONE, SPECIFIC THING I WILL WORK TO IMPROVE NEXT SESSION

| CREATE A SIGNATURE YOU LOVE • PHASE TWO WORKBOOK PAPER

Write down your observations and your one, specific goal for next session in the space below.

| POSITIVES

| NEEDS IMPROVEMENT

| ONE, SPECIFIC THING I WILL WORK TO IMPROVE NEXT SESSION

CREATE A SIGNATURE YOU LOVE • PHASE TWO WORKBOOK PAPER

Write down your observations and your one, specific goal for next session in the space below.

POSITIVES

NEEDS IMPROVEMENT

ONE, SPECIFIC THING I WILL WORK TO IMPROVE NEXT SESSION

Write down your observations and your one, specific goal for next session in the space below.

| POSITIVES

| NEEDS IMPROVEMENT

| ONE, SPECIFIC THING I WILL WORK TO IMPROVE NEXT SESSION

Write down your observations and your one, specific goal for next session in the space below.

| POSITIVES

| NEEDS IMPROVEMENT

| ONE, SPECIFIC THING I WILL WORK TO IMPROVE NEXT SESSION

Write down your observations and your one, specific goal for next session in the space below.

| POSITIVES

| NEEDS IMPROVEMENT

| ONE, SPECIFIC THING I WILL WORK TO IMPROVE NEXT
SESSION

Write down your observations and your one, specific goal for next session in the space below.

| POSITIVES

| NEEDS IMPROVEMENT

| ONE, SPECIFIC THING I WILL WORK TO IMPROVE NEXT SESSION

Write down your observations and your one, specific goal for next session in the space below.

| POSITIVES

| NEEDS IMPROVEMENT

| ONE, SPECIFIC THING I WILL WORK TO IMPROVE NEXT SESSION

| CREATE A SIGNATURE YOU LOVE · PHASE TWO WORKBOOK PAPER

Write down your observations and your one, specific goal for next session in the space below.

| POSITIVES

| NEEDS IMPROVEMENT

| ONE, SPECIFIC THING I WILL WORK TO IMPROVE NEXT SESSION

| POSITIVES

| NEEDS IMPROVEMENT

| ONE, SPECIFIC THING I WILL WORK TO IMPROVE NEXT SESSION

Write down your observations and your one, specific goal for next session in the space below.

| POSITIVES

| NEEDS IMPROVEMENT

Write down your observations and your one, specific goal for next session in the space below.

| ONE, SPECIFIC THING I WILL WORK TO IMPROVE NEXT SESSION

Write down your observations and your one, specific goal for next session in the space below.

| POSITIVES

| NEEDS IMPROVEMENT

| ONE, SPECIFIC THING I WILL WORK TO IMPROVE NEXT SESSION

CREATE A SIGNATURE YOU LOVE · PHASE TWO WORKBOOK PAPER

| POSITIVES

| NEEDS IMPROVEMENT

Write down your observations and your one, specific goal for next session in the space below.

| ONE, SPECIFIC THING I WILL WORK TO IMPROVE NEXT SESSION

Phase Three Workbook Paper

Write down your observations and your one, specific goal for next session in the space below.

POSITIVES

NEEDS IMPROVEMENT

ONE, SPECIFIC THING I WILL WORK TO IMPROVE NEXT SESSION

✂

CREATE A SIGNATURE YOU LOVE • PHASE THREE WORKBOOK PAPER

Write down your observations and your one, specific goal for next session in the space below.

| POSITIVES

| NEEDS IMPROVEMENT

| ONE, SPECIFIC THING I WILL WORK TO IMPROVE NEXT SESSION

| CREATE A SIGNATURE YOU LOVE • PHASE THREE WORKBOOK PAPER

Write down your observations and your one, specific goal for next session in the space below.

| POSITIVES

| NEEDS IMPROVEMENT

| ONE, SPECIFIC THING I WILL WORK TO IMPROVE NEXT SESSION

CREATE A SIGNATURE YOU LOVE • PHASE THREE WORKBOOK PAPER

Write down your observations and your one, specific goal for next session in the space below.

POSITIVES

NEEDS IMPROVEMENT

ONE, SPECIFIC THING I WILL WORK TO IMPROVE NEXT SESSION

| CREATE A SIGNATURE YOU LOVE • PHASE THREE WORKBOOK PAPER

Write down your observations and your one, specific goal for next session in the space below.

| POSITIVES

| NEEDS IMPROVEMENT

| ONE, SPECIFIC THING I WILL WORK TO IMPROVE NEXT SESSION

| POSITIVES

| NEEDS IMPROVEMENT

| ONE, SPECIFIC THING I WILL WORK TO IMPROVE NEXT SESSION

Write down your observations and your one, specific goal for next session in the space below.

Write down your observations and your one, specific goal for next session in the space below.

| POSITIVES

| NEEDS IMPROVEMENT

| ONE, SPECIFIC THING I WILL WORK TO IMPROVE NEXT SESSION

CREATE A SIGNATURE YOU LOVE · PHASE THREE WORKBOOK PAPER

Write down your observations and your one, specific goal for next session in the space below.

| POSITIVES

| NEEDS IMPROVEMENT

| ONE, SPECIFIC THING I WILL WORK TO IMPROVE NEXT SESSION

| CREATE A SIGNATURE YOU LOVE • PHASE THREE WORKBOOK PAPER

Write down your observations and your one, specific goal for next session in the space below.

| POSITIVES

| NEEDS IMPROVEMENT

| ONE, SPECIFIC THING I WILL WORK TO IMPROVE NEXT SESSION

✂

CREATE A SIGNATURE YOU LOVE · PHASE THREE WORKBOOK PAPER

Write down your observations and your one, specific goal for next session in the space below.

| POSITIVES

| NEEDS IMPROVEMENT

| ONE, SPECIFIC THING I WILL WORK TO IMPROVE NEXT SESSION

| CREATE A SIGNATURE YOU LOVE • PHASE THREE WORKBOOK PAPER

Write down your observations and your one, specific goal for next session in the space below.

| POSITIVES

| NEEDS IMPROVEMENT

| ONE, SPECIFIC THING I WILL WORK TO IMPROVE NEXT SESSION

| POSITIVES | NEEDS IMPROVEMENT | ONE, SPECIFIC THING I WILL WORK TO IMPROVE NEXT SESSION |

Write down your observations and your one, specific goal for next session in the space below.

Write down your observations and your one, specific goal for next session in the space below.

| POSITIVES

| NEEDS IMPROVEMENT

| ONE, SPECIFIC THING I WILL WORK TO IMPROVE NEXT SESSION

CREATE A SIGNATURE YOU LOVE · PHASE THREE WORKBOOK PAPER

Write down your observations and your one, specific goal for next session in the space below.

| POSITIVES

| NEEDS IMPROVEMENT

| ONE, SPECIFIC THING I WILL WORK TO IMPROVE NEXT SESSION

Write down your observations and your one, specific goal for next session in the space below.

| POSITIVES

| NEEDS IMPROVEMENT

| ONE, SPECIFIC THING I WILL WORK TO IMPROVE NEXT SESSION

| CREATE A SIGNATURE YOU LOVE ∙ PHASE THREE WORKBOOK PAPER

Write down your observations and your one, specific goal for next session in the space below.

| POSITIVES

| NEEDS IMPROVEMENT

| ONE, SPECIFIC THING I WILL WORK TO IMPROVE NEXT SESSION

Font Index

Alice

ABCDEFGHIJKLMNOPQRSTUVWXYZ
abcdefghijklmnopqrstuvwxyz

Alice-Regular.ttf: Copyright (c) 2011 The Alice Project Authors (contact@cyreal.org) with Reserved Font Name "Alice"

This Font Software is licensed under the SIL Open Font License, Version 1.1.This license is copied at page 181, and is also available with a FAQ athttp://scripts.sil.org/OFL.

Baumans

ABCDEFGHIJKLMNOPQRSTUVWXYZ
abcdefghijklmnopqrstuvwxyz

Baumans-Regular.ttf: Copyright (c) 2011, Cyreal (www.cyreal.org) with Reserved Font Name "Baumans".

This Font Software is licensed under the SIL Open Font License, Version 1.1.This license is copied at page 181, and is also available with a FAQ athttp://scripts.sil.org/OFL.

Amarante

ABCDEFGHIJKLMNOPQRSTUVWXYZ
abcdefghijklmnopqrstuvwxyz

Amarante-Regular.ttf: Copyright (c) 2011, Sorkin Type Co (www.sorkintype.com) with Reserved Font Name "Amarante".

This Font Software is licensed under the SIL Open Font License, Version 1.1. This license is copied at page 181, and is also available with a FAQ athttp://scripts.sil.org/OFL.

Glass Antiqua

ABCDEFGHIJKLMNOPQRSTUVWXYZ
abcdefghijklmnopqrstuvwxyz

GlassAntiqua-Regular.ttf: Copyright (c) 2011, Denis Masharov <denis.masharov@gmail.com>.

This Font Software is licensed under the SIL Open Font License, Version 1.1. This license is copied at page 181, and is also available with a FAQ at http://scripts.sil.org/OFL.

Amatic SC

ABCDEFGHIJKLMNOPQRSTUVWXYZ
ABCDEFGHIJKLMNOPQRSTUVWXYZ

AmaticSC-Regular.ttf: Copyright 2015 The Amatic SC Project Authors (https://github.com/googlefonts/AmaticSC)

This Font Software is licensed under the SIL Open Font License, Version 1.1. This license is copied at page 181, and is also available with a FAQ at http://scripts.sil.org/OFL.

Amita

ABCDEFGHIJKLMNOPQRSTUVWXYZ
abcdefghijklmnopqrstuvwxyz

Amita-Regular.ttf: Copyright (c) 2014, Eduardo Rodriguez Tunni. Copyright (c) 2000, Modular Infotech, Pune, INDIA. All rights reserved. Copyright (c) 2011 by Brian J. Bonislawsky DBA Astigmatic (AOETI) (astigma@astigmatic.com). All rights reserved. This Font Software is licensed under the SIL Open Font License, Version 1.1. This license is copied at page 181, and is also available with a FAQ at http://scripts.sil.org/OFL.

Lancelot

ABCDEFGHIJKLMNOPQRSTUVWXYZ
abcdefghijklmnopqrstuvwxyz

Lancelot-Regular.ttf: Copyright (c) 2011 by Marion Kadi (marionkadi@gmail.com). All rights reserved.
This Font Software is licensed under the SIL Open Font License, Version 1.1. This license is copied at page 181, and is also available with a FAQ at http://scripts.sil.org/OFL.

Montserrat Alternates

ABCDEFGHIJKLMNOPQRSTUVWXYZ
abcdefghijklmnopqrstuvwxyz

MontserratAlternates-Regular.ttf: Copyright 2011 The Montserrat Project Authors (https://github.com/JulietaUla/Montserrat)
This Font Software is licensed under the SIL Open Font License, Version 1.1. This license is copied at page 181, and is also available with a FAQ at http://scripts.sil.org/OFL.

Playball

ABCDEFGHIJKLMNOPQRSTUVWXYZ
abcdefghijklmnopqrstuvwxyz

Playball-Regular.ttf: Copyright (c) 2011 TypeSETit, LLC (typesetit@att.net), with Reserved Font Name "Playball"
This Font Software is licensed under the SIL Open Font License, Version 1.1. This license is copied at page 181, and is also available with a FAQ at http://scripts.sil.org/OFL.

Warnes

ABCDEFGHIJKLMNOPQRSTUVWXYZ
abcdefghijklmnopqrstuvwxyz

Warnes-Regular.ttf: Copyright (c) 2012, Eduardo Tunni (http://www.tipo.net.ar), with Reserved Font Name 'Warnes'
This Font Software is licensed under the SIL Open Font License, Version 1.1. This license is copied at page 181, and is also available with a FAQ at http://scripts.sil.org/OFL.

Sofadi One

ABCDEFGHIJKLMNOPQRSTUVWXYZ
abcdefghijklmnopqrstuvwxyz

SofadiOne-Regular.ttf: Copyright (c) 2011 by Botjo Nikoltchev, with Reserved Font Name 'Sofadi One'

This Font Software is licensed under the SIL Open Font License, Version 1.1. This license is copied at page 181, and is also available with a FAQ at http://scripts.sil.org/OFL.

Romanesco

ABCDEFGHIJKLMNOPQRSTUVWXYZ
abcdefghijklmnopqrstuvwxyz

Romanesco-Regular.ttf: Copyright (c) 2012 by Brian J. Bonislawsky DBA Astigmatic (AOETI) (astigma@astigmatic.com), with Reserved Font Name "Romanesco"

This Font Software is licensed under the SIL Open Font License, Version 1.1. This license is copied at page 181, and is also available with a FAQ at http://scripts.sil.org/OFL.

Macondo

ABCDEFGHIJKLMNOPQRSTUVWXYZ
abcdefghijklmnopqrstuvwxyz

Macondo-Regular.ttf: Copyright (c) 1997 - 2011, John Vargas Beltran. (www.johnvargasbeltran.com|john.vargasbeltran@gmail.com), with Reserved Font Name "Macondo"

This Font Software is licensed under the SIL Open Font License, Version 1.1. This license is copied at page 181, and is also available with a FAQ at http://scripts.sil.org/OFL.

Nothing You Could Do

ABCDEFGHIJKLMNOPQRSTUVWXYZ
abcdefghijklmnopqrstuvwxyz

NothingYouCouldDo.ttf: Copyright (c) 2010, Kimberly Geswein (kimberlygeswein.com).

This Font Software is licensed under the SIL Open Font License, Version 1.1. This license is copied at page 181, and is also available with a FAQ at http://scripts.sil.org/OFL.

Nova Script

ABCDEFGHIJKLMNOPQRSTUVWXYZ
abcdefghijklmnopqrstuvwxyz

NovaScript-Regular.ttf: Copyright (c) 2011, wmk69 (wmk69@o2.pl) with Reserved Font Names 'NovaScript' and 'Nova Script'

This Font Software is licensed under the SIL Open Font License, Version 1.1. This license is copied at page 181, and is also available with a FAQ at http://scripts.sil.org/OFL.

Bilbo

ABCDEFGHIJKLMNOPQRSTUVWXYZ
abcdefghijklmnopqrstuvwxyz

Bilbo-Regular.ttf: Copyright (c) 2011 TypeSETit, LLC (typesetit@att.net), with Reserved Font Name "Bilbo"

This Font Software is licensed under the SIL Open Font License, Version 1.1. This license is copied at page 181, and is also available with a FAQ at http://scripts.sil.org/OFL.

Covered By Your Grace

ABCDEFGHIJKLMNOPQRSTUVWXYZ
abcdefghijklmnopqrstuvwxyz

CoveredByYourGrace.ttf: Copyright (c) 2010, Kimberly Geswein (kimberlygeswein.com)

This Font Software is licensed under the SIL Open Font License, Version 1.1. This license is copied at page 181, and is also available with a FAQ at http://scripts.sil.org/OFL.

Give You Glory

ABCDEFGHIJKLMNOPQRSTUVWXYZ
abcdefghijklmnopqrstuvwxyz

GiveYouGlory.ttf: Copyright (c) 2010, Kimberly Geswein (kimberlygeswein.com).

This Font Software is licensed under the SIL Open Font License, Version 1.1. This license is copied at page 181, and is also available with a FAQ at http://scripts.sil.org/OFL.

Bad Script

ABCDEFGHIJKLMNOPQRSTUVWXYZ
abcdefghijklmnopqrstuvwxyz

BadScript-Regular.ttf: Copyright (c) 2011, Cyreal (www.cyreal.org) with Reserved Font Name "Bad Script".

This Font Software is licensed under the SIL Open Font License, Version 1.1. This license is copied at page 181, and is also available with a FAQ at http://scripts.sil.org/OFL.

Julee

ABCDEFGHIJKLMNOPQRSTUVWXYZ
abcdefghijklmnopqrstuvwxyz

Julee-Regular.ttf: Copyright (c) 2011, Julian Tunni (jotadejulian@hotmail.com), with Reserved Font Name "Julee".

This Font Software is licensed under the SIL Open Font License, Version 1.1. This license is copied at page 181, and is also available with a FAQ at http://scripts.sil.org/OFL.

Crafty Girls

ABCDEFGHIJKLMNOPQRSTUVWXYZ
abcdefghijklmnopqrstuvwxyz

CraftyGirls-Regular.ttf: Copyright (c) 2010 by Font Diner, Inc DBA Tart Workshop. All rights reserved.

Licensed under the Apache License, Version 2.0 (the "License"); you may not use this file except in compliance with the License. You may obtain a copy of the License on page 182 of this book or at http://www.apache.org/licenses/LICENSE-2.0

Unless required by applicable law or agreed to in writing, software distributed under the License is distributed on an "AS IS" BASIS, WITHOUT WARRANTIES OR CONDITIONS OF ANY KIND, either express or implied. See the License for the specific language governing permissions and limitations under the License.

Zeyada

ABCDEFGHIJKLMNOPQRSTUVWXYZ
abcdefghijklmnopqrstuvwxyz

Zeyada.ttf: Copyright (c) 2010, Kimberly Geswein (kimberlygeswein.com)

This Font Software is licensed under the SIL Open Font License, Version 1.1. This license is copied at page 181, and is also available with a FAQ at http://scripts.sil.org/OFL.

Allura

ABCDEFGHIJKLMNOPQRSTUVWXYZ
abcdefghijklmnopqrstuvwxyz

Allura-Regular.ttf: Copyright (c) 2011 TypeSETit, LLC (typesetit@ att.net), with Reserved Font Name "Allura"

This Font Software is licensed under the SIL Open Font License, Version 1.1. This license is copied at page 181, and is also available with a FAQ at http://scripts.sil.org/OFL.

Grand Hotel

ABCDEFGHIJKLMNOPQRSTUVWXYZ
abcdefghijklmnopqrstuvwxyz

GrandHotel-Regular.ttf: Copyright (c) 2012 by Brian J. Bonislawsky DBA Astigmatic (AOETI) (astigma@astigmatic. com), with Reserved Font Name "Grand Hotel"

This Font Software is licensed under the SIL Open Font License, Version 1.1. This license is copied at page 181, and is also available with a FAQ at http://scripts.sil.org/OFL.

Sunshiney

ABCDEFGHIJKLMNOPQRSTUVWXYZ
abcdefghijklmnopqrstuvwxyz

Sunshiney-Regular.ttf: Copyright (c) 2010 by Font Diner, Inc DBA Sideshow. All rights reserved.

Licensed under the Apache License, Version 2.0 (the "License"); you may not use this file except in compliance with the License. You may obtain a copy of the License on page 182 of this book or at http://www.apache.org/licenses/LICENSE-2.0

Unless required by applicable law or agreed to in writing, software distributed under the License is distributed on an "AS IS" BASIS, WITHOUT WARRANTIES OR CONDITIONS OF ANY KIND, either express or implied. See the License for the specific language governing permissions andlimitations under the License.

Spirax

ABCDEFGHIJKLMNOPQRSTUVWXYZ
abcdefghijklmnopqrstuvwxyz

Spirax-Regular.ttf: Copyright (c) 2011 by Brenda Gallo (gbrenda1987@gmail.com), with Reserved Font Name Spirax.

Stalemate

ABCDEFGHIJKLMNOPQRSTUVWXYZ
abcdefghijklmnopqrstuvwxyz

Stalemate-Regular.ttf: Copyright (c) 2012 by Jim Lyles for Astigmatic (AOETI) (astigma@astigmatic.com), with Reserved Font Name 'Stalemate'

This Font Software is licensed under the SIL Open Font License, Version 1.1. This license is copied at page 181, and is also available with a FAQ at http://scripts.sil.org/OFL.

Kristi

ABCDEFGHIJKLMNOPQRSTUVWXYZ
abcdefghijklmnopqrstuvwxyz

Kristi-Regular.ttf: Copyright (c) 2010, Birgit Pulk (birgitpulk@gmail.com). All rights reserved.

This Font Software is licensed under the SIL Open Font License, Version 1.1. This license is copied at page 181, and is also available with a FAQ at http://scripts.sil.org/OFL.

La Belle Aurore

ABCDEFGHIJKLMNOPQRSTUVWXYZ
abcdefghijklmnopqrstuvwxyz

LaBelleAurore.ttf: Copyright (c) 2010, Kimberly Geswein (kimberlygeswein.com kimberlygeswein@gmail.com)

This Font Software is licensed under the SIL Open Font License, Version 1.1. This license is copied at page 181, and is also available with a FAQ at http://scripts.sil.org/OFL.

Dawning of a New Day

ABCDEFGHIJKLMNOPQRSTUVWXYZ
abcdefghyklmnopqrstuvwxyz

DawningofaNewDay.ttf: Copyright (c) 2010, Kimberly Geswein (kimberlygeswein.com)

This Font Software is licensed under the SIL Open Font License, Version 1.1. This license is copied at page 181, and is also available with a FAQ at http://scripts.sil.org/OFL.

Arizonia

ABCDEFGHIJKLMNOPQRSTUVWXYZ
abcdefghijklmnopqrstuvwxyz

Arizonia-Regular.ttf: Copyright (c) 2011 TypeSETit, LLC (typesetit@att.net), with Reserved Font Name "Arizonia"

This Font Software is licensed under the SIL Open Font License, Version 1.1. This license is copied at page 181, and is also available with a FAQ at http://scripts.sil.org/OFL.

Bonbon

$\mathcal{ABCDEFGHIJKLMNOPQRSTUVWXYZ}$
$abcdefghijklmnopqrstuvwxyz$

Bonbon-Regular.ttf: Copyright (c) 2011, Cyreal (www.cyreal.org) with Reserved Font Name "Bonbon".

This Font Software is licensed under the SIL Open Font License, Version 1.1. This license is copied at page 181, and is also available with a FAQ at http://scripts.sil.org/OFL.

Cherry Swash

ABCDEFGHIJKLMNOPQRSTUVWXYZ
abcdefghijklmnopqrstuvwxyz

CherrySwash-Regular.ttf: Copyright (c) 2012, Natalia Kasatkina (kasatkinanataliya@gmail.com)

This Font Software is licensed under the SIL Open Font License, Version 1.1. This license is copied at page 181, and is also available with a FAQ at http://scripts.sil.org/OFL.

Princess Sofia

ABCDEFGHIJKLMNOPQRSTUVWXYZ
abcdefghijklmnopqrstuvwxyz

PrincessSofia-Regular.ttf: Copyright (c) 2012 by Font Diner, Inc DBA Tart Workshop (diner@fontdiner.com) with Reserved Font Name "Princess Sofia"

This Font Software is licensed under the SIL Open Font License, Version 1.1. This license is copied at page 181, and is also available with a FAQ at http://scripts.sil.org/OFL.

Sacramento

ABCDEFGHIJKLMNOPQRSTUVWXYZ
abcdefghijklmnopqrstuvwxyz

Sacramento-Regular.ttf: Copyright (c) 2012 by Brian J. Bonislawsky DBA Astigmatic (AOETI) (astigma@astigmatic.com), with Reserved Font Name 'Sacramento'

This Font Software is licensed under the SIL Open Font License, Version 1.1. This license is copied at page 181, and is also available with a FAQ at http://scripts.sil.org/OFL.

Mr Bedfort

ABCDEFGHIJKLMNOPQRSTUVWXYZ
abcdefghijklmnopqrstuvwxyz

MrBedfort-Regular.ttf: Copyright (c) 2006 Alejandro Paul (sudtipos@sudtipos.com), with Reserved Font Name "Mr Bedfort"

This Font Software is licensed under the SIL Open Font License, Version 1.1. This license is copied at page 181, and is also available with a FAQ at http://scripts.sil.org/OFL.

Herr Von Mullerhoff

ABCDEFGHIJKLMNOPQRSTUVWXYZ
abcdefghijklmnopqrstuvwxyz

HerrVonMuellerhoff-Regular.ttf: Copyright (c) 2004 Alejandro Paul (sudtipos@sudtipos.com), with Reserved Font Name "Herr Von Mullerhoff"

Engagement

ABCDEFGHIJKLMNOPQRSTUVWXYZ
abcdefghijklmnopqrstuvwxyz

Engagement-Regular.ttf: Copyright (c) 2011 by Brian J. Bonislawsky DBA Astigmatic (AOETI) (astigma@astigmatic.com), with Reserved Font Name "Engagement"

This Font Software is licensed under the SIL Open Font License, Version 1.1. This license is copied at page 181, and is also available with a FAQ at http://scripts.sil.org/OFL.

Parisienne

ABCDEFGHIJKLMNOPQRSTUVWXYZ
abcdefghijklmnopqrstuvwxyz

Parisienne-Regular.ttf: Copyright (c) 2012 by Brian J. Bonislawsky DBA Astigmatic (AOETI) (astigma@astigmatic.com), with Reserved Font Name "Parisienne"

This Font Software is licensed under the SIL Open Font License, Version 1.1. This license is copied at page 181, and is also available with a FAQ at http://scripts.sil.org/OFL.

Rochester

ABCDEFGHIJKLMNOPQRSTUVWXYZ
abcdefghijklmnopqrstuvwxyz

Rochester-Regular.ttf: Copyright (c) 2010 by Font Diner, Inc DBA Sideshow. All rights reserved.

Licensed under the Apache License, Version 2.0 (the "License"); you may not use this file except in compliance with the License. You may obtain a copy of the License on page 182 of this book or at http://www.apache.org/licenses/LICENSE-2.0

Unless required by applicable law or agreed to in writing, software distributed under the License is distributed on an "AS IS" BASIS, WITHOUT WARRANTIES OR CONDITIONS OF ANY KIND, either express or implied. See the License for the specific language governing permissions andlimitations under the License.

Meie Script

ABCDEFGHIJKLMNOPQRSTUVWXYZ
abcdefghijklmnopqrstuvwxyz

MeieScript-Regular.ttf: Copyright (c) 2011, 2012 Johan Kallas (johankallas@gmail.com), Mihkel Virkus (mihkelvirkus@gmail.com), with Reserved Font Name 'Meie Script'

This Font Software is licensed under the SIL Open Font License, Version 1.1. This license is copied at page 181, and is also available with a FAQ at http://scripts.sil.org/OFL.

Milonga

ABCDEFGHIJKLMNOPQRSTUVWXYZ
abcdefghijklmnopqrstuvwxyz

Milonga-Regular.ttf: Copyright (c) 2011, Pablo Impallari (www.impallari.com|impallari@gmail.com), Copyright (c) 2011, Brenda Gallo (gbrenda1987@gmail.com), Copyright (c) 2011, Rodrigo Fuenzalida (www.rfuenzalida.com|hello@rfuenzalida.com), with Reserved Font Name Milonga.

This Font Software is licensed under the SIL Open Font License, Version 1.1. This license is copied at page 181, and is also available with a FAQ at http://scripts.sil.org/OFL.

Miss Fajardoe

ABCDEFGHIJKLMNOPQRSTUVWXYZ
abcdefghijklmnopqrstuvwxyz

MissFajardose-Regular.ttf: Copyright (c) 2004 Alejandro Paul (sudtipos@sudtipos.com), with Reserved Font Name "MissFajardose"

This Font Software is licensed under the SIL Open Font License, Version 1.1. This license is copied at page 181, and is also available with a FAQ at http://scripts.sil.org/OFL.

Macondo Swash Caps

ABCDEFGHIJKLMNOPQRSTUVWXYZ
abcdefghijklmnopqrstuvwxyz

MacondoSwashCaps-Regular.ttf: Copyright (c) 1997 - 2011, John Vargas Beltran. (www.johnvargasbeltran.com|john.vargasbeltran@gmail.com), with Reserved Font Name "Macondo"

This Font Software is licensed under the SIL Open Font License, Version 1.1. This license is copied at 181, and is also available with a FAQ at http://scripts.sil.org/OFL.

Marck Script

ABCDEFGHIJKLMNOPQRSTUVWXYZ
abcdefghijklmnopqrstuvwxyz

MarckScript-Regular.ttf: Copyright (c) 2011, Denis Masharov <denis.masharov@gmail.com>, Marck Fogel, with Reserved Font Names "Marck Script".

This Font Software is licensed under the SIL Open Font License, Version 1.1. This license is copied at page 181, and is also available with a FAQ at http://scripts.sil.org/OFL.

Meddon

ABCDEFGHIJKLMNOPQRSTUVWXYZ
abcdefghijklmnopqrstuvwxyz

Meddon.ttf: Copyright (c) 2011 by Vernon Adams (vern@newtypography.co.uk) with Reserved Font Name 'Meddon'. All rights reserved.

Euphoria Script

ABCDEFGHIJKLMNOPQRSTUVWXYZ
abcdefghijklmnopqrstuvwxyz

EuphoriaScript-Regular.ttf: Copyright (c) 2012 Sabrina Mariela Lopez (typesenses@live.com.ar), with Reserved Font Name "Euphoria Script"

This Font Software is licensed under the SIL Open Font License, Version 1.1. This license is copied at page 181, and is also available with a FAQ at http://scripts.sil.org/OFL.

Great Vibes

ABCDEFGHIJKLMNOPQRSTUVWXYZ
abcdefghijklmnopqrstuvwxyz

GreatVibes-Regular.ttf: Copyright (c) 2012 TypeSETit, LLC (typesetit@att.net), with Reserved Font Name "Great Vibes"

This Font Software is licensed under the SIL Open Font License, Version 1.1. This license is copied at page 181, and is also available with a FAQ at http://scripts.sil.org/OFL.

Aguafina Script

ABCDEFGHIJKLMNOPQRSTUVWXYZ
abcdefghijklmnopqrstuvwxyz

AguafinaScript-Regular.ttf: Copyright (c) 2007 Angel Koziupa (sudtipos@sudtipos.com), Copyright (c) 2007 Alejandro Paul (sudtipos@sudtipos.com), with Reserved Font Name "Aguafina Script"

This Font Software is licensed under the SIL Open Font License, Version 1.1. This license is copied at page 181, and is also available with a FAQ at http://scripts.sil.org/OFL.

Alex Brush

ABCDEFGHIJKLMNOPQRSTUVWXYZ
abcdefghijklmnopqrstuvwxyz

AlexBrush-Regular.ttf: Copyright (c) 2011 TypeSETit, LLC (typesetit@att.net), with Reserved Font Name "Alex Brush"

This Font Software is licensed under the SIL Open Font License, Version 1.1. This license is copied at page 181, and is also available with a FAQ at http://scripts.sil.org/OFL.

Cinzel Decorative

ABCDEFGHIJKLMNOPQRSTUVWXYZ
ABCDEFGHIJKLMNOPQRSTUVWXYZ

CinzelDecorative-Regular.ttf: Copyright 2012 Natanael Gama (info@ndiscovered.com), with Reserved Font Name 'Cinzel'

This Font Software is licensed under the SIL Open Font License, Version 1.1. This license is copied at page 181, and is also available with a FAQ at http://scripts.sil.org/OFL.

Dynalight

ABCDEFGHIJKLMNOPQRSTUVWXYZ
abcdefghijklmnopqrstuvwxyz

Dynalight-Regular.ttf: Copyright (c) 2011 by Brian J. Bonislawsky DBA Astigmatic (AOETI) (astigma@astigmatic.com), with Reserved Font Name "Dynalight"

This Font Software is licensed under the SIL Open Font License, Version 1.1. This license is copied at page 181, and is also available with a FAQ at http://scripts.sil.org/OFL.

Sil Open Font License

Version 1.1 - 26 February 2007

• **PREAMBLE.** The goals of the Open Font License (OFL) are to stimulate worldwide development of collaborative font projects, to support the font creation efforts of academic and linguistic communities, and to provide a free and open framework in which fonts may be shared and improved in partnership with others. The OFL allows the licensed fonts to be used, studied, modified and redistributed freely as long as they are not sold by themselves. The fonts, including any derivative works, can be bundled, embedded, redistributed anwWd/or sold with any software provided that any reserved names are not used by derivative works. The fonts and derivatives, however, cannot be released under any other type of license. The requirement for fonts to remain under this license does not apply to any document created using the fonts or their derivatives. • **DEFINITIONS.** "Font Software" refers to the set of files released by the Copyright Holder(s) under this license and clearly marked as such. This mayinclude source files, build scripts and documentation. / "Reserved Font Name" refers to any names specified as such after the copyright statement(s). / "Original Version" refers to the collection of Font Software components as distributed by the Copyright Holder(s). / "Modified Version" refers to any derivative made by adding to, deleting, or substituting - in part or in whole - any of the components of the Original Version, by changing formats or by porting the Font Software to a new environment. / "Author" refers to any designer, engineer, programmer, technical writer or other person who contributed to the Font Software. • **PERMISSION & CONDITIONS.** Permission is hereby granted, free of charge, to any person obtaining a copy of the Font Software, to use, study, copy, merge, embed, modify, redistribute, and sell modified and unmodified copies of the Font Software, subject to the following conditions: 1) Neither the Font Software nor any of its individual components, in Original or Modified Versions, may be sold by itself. / 2) Original or Modified Versions of the Font Software may be bundled, redistributed and/or sold with any software, provided that each copy contains the above copyright notice and this license. These can be included either as stand-alone text files, human-readable headers or in the appropriate machine-readable metadata fields within text or binary files as long as those fields can be easily viewed by the user. / 3) No Modified Version of the Font Software may use the Reserved Font Name(s) unless explicit written permission is granted by the corresponding Copyright Holder. This restriction only applies to the primary font name as presented to the users. / 4) The name(s) of the Copyright Holder(s) or the Author(s) of the Font Software shall not be used to promote, endorse or advertise any Modified Version, except to acknowledge the contribution(s) of the Copyright Holder(s) and the Author(s) or with their explicit written permission. / 5) The Font Software, modified or unmodified, in part or in whole, must be distributed entirely under this license, and must not be distributed under any other license. The requirement for fonts to remain under this license does not apply to any document created using the Font Software. • **TERMINATION.** This license becomes null and void if any of the above conditions are not met. • **DISCLAIMER.** THE FONT SOFTWARE IS PROVIDED "AS IS", WITHOUT WARRANTY OF ANY KIND, EXPRESS OR IMPLIED, INCLUDING BUT NOT LIMITED TO ANY WARRANTIES OF MERCHANTABILITY, FITNESS FOR A PARTICULAR PURPOSE AND NONINFRINGEMENT OF COPYRIGHT, PATENT, TRADEMARK, OR OTHER RIGHT. IN NO EVENT SHALL THE COPYRIGHT HOLDER BE LIABLE FOR ANY CLAIM, DAMAGES OR OTHER LIABILITY, INCLUDING ANY GENERAL, SPECIAL, INDIRECT, INCIDENTAL, OR CONSEQUENTIAL DAMAGES, WHETHER IN AN ACTION OF CONTRACT, TORT OR OTHERWISE, ARISING FROM, OUT OF THE USE OR INABILITY TO USE THE FONT SOFTWARE OR FROM OTHER DEALINGS IN THE FONT SOFTWARE.

Apache License Version 2.0

January 2004 http://www.apache.org/licenses/ TERMS AND CONDITIONS FOR USE, REPRODUCTION, AND DISTRIBUTION

• **1. DEFINITIONS.** "License" shall mean the terms and conditions for use, reproduction, and distribution as defined by Sections 1 through 9 of this document. "Licensor" shall mean the copyright owner or entity authorized by the copyright owner that is granting the License. "Legal Entity" shall mean the union of the acting entity and all other entities that control, are controlled by, or are under common control with that entity. For the purposes of this definition, "control" means (i) the power, direct or indirect, to cause the direction or management of such entity, whether by contract or otherwise, or (ii) ownership of fifty percent (50%) or more of the outstanding shares, or (iii) beneficial ownership of such entity. "You" (or "Your") shall mean an individual or Legal Entity exercising permissions granted by this License. "Source" form shall mean the preferred form for making modifications, including but not limited to software source code, documentation source, and configuration files. "Object" form shall mean any form resulting from mechanical transformation or translation of a Source form, including but not limited to compiled object code, generated documentation, and conversions to other media types. "Work" shall mean the work of authorship, whether in Source or Object form, made available under the License, as indicated by a copyright notice that is included in or attached to the work (an example is provided in the Appendix below). "Derivative Works" shall mean any work, whether in Source or Object form, that is based on (or derived from) the Work and for which the editorial revisions, annotations, elaborations, or other modifications represent, as a whole, an original work of authorship. For the purposes of this License, Derivative Works shall not include works that remain separable from, or merely link (or bind by name) to the interfaces of, the Work and Derivative Works thereof. "Contribution" shall mean any work of authorship, including the original version of the Work and any modifications or additions to that Work or Derivative Works thereof, that is intentionally submitted to Licensor for inclusion in the Work by the copyright owner or by an individual or Legal Entity authorized to submit on behalf of the copyright owner. For the purposes of this definition, "submitted" means any form of electronic, verbal, or written communication sent to the Licensor or its representatives, including but not limited to communication on electronic mailing lists, source code control systems, and issue tracking systems that are managed by, or on behalf of, the Licensor for the purpose of discussing and improving the Work, but excluding communication that is conspicuously marked or otherwise designated in writing by the copyright owner as "Not a Contribution." "Contributor" shall mean Licensor and any individual or Legal Entity on behalf of whom a Contribution has been received by Licensor and subsequently incorporated within the Work. • **2. GRANT OF COPYRIGHT LICENSE.** Subject to the terms and conditions of this License, each Contributor hereby grants to You a perpetual, worldwide, non-exclusive, no-charge, royalty-free, irrevocable copyright license to reproduce, prepare Derivative Works of, publicly display, publicly perform, sublicense, and distribute the Work and such Derivative Works in Source or Object form. • **3. GRANT OF PATENT LICENSE.** Subject to the terms and conditions of this License, each Contributor hereby grants to You a perpetual, worldwide, non-exclusive, no-charge, royalty-free, irrevocable (except as stated in this section) patent license to make, have made, use, offer to sell, sell, import, and otherwise transfer the Work, where such license applies only to those patent claims licensable by such Contributor that are necessarily infringed by their Contribution(s) alone or by combination of their Contribution(s) with the Work to which such Contribution(s) was submitted. If You institute patent litigation against any entity (including a cross-claim or counterclaim in a lawsuit) alleging that the Work or a Contribution incorporated within the Work constitutes direct or contributory patent infringement, then any patent licenses granted to You under this

License for that Work shall terminate as of the date such litigation is filed. • **4. REDISTRIBUTION.** You may reproduce and distribute copies of the Work or Derivative Works thereof in any medium, with or without modifications, and in Source or Object form, provided that You meet the following conditions: (a) You must give any other recipients of the Work or Derivative Works a copy of this License; and (b) You must cause any modified files to carry prominent notices stating that You changed the files; and (c) You must retain, in the Source form of any Derivative Works that You distribute, all copyright, patent, trademark, and attribution notices from the Source form of the Work, excluding those notices that do not pertain to any part of the Derivative Works; and (d) If the Work includes a "NOTICE" text file as part of its distribution, then any Derivative Works that You distribute must include a readable copy of the attribution notices contained within such NOTICE file, excluding those notices that do not pertain to any part of the Derivative Works, in at least one of the following places: within a NOTICE text file distributed as part of the Derivative Works; within the Source form or documentation, if provided along with the Derivative Works; or, within a display generated by the Derivative Works, if and wherever such third-party notices normally appear. The contents of the NOTICE file are for informational purposes only and do not modify the License. You may add Your own attribution notices within Derivative Works that You distribute, alongside or as an addendum to the NOTICE text from the Work, provided that such additional attribution notices cannot be construed as modifying the License. You may add Your own copyright statement to Your modifications and may provide additional or different license terms and conditions for use, reproduction, or distribution of Your modifications, or for any such Derivative Works as a whole, provided Your use, reproduction, and distribution of the Work otherwise complies with the conditions stated in this License. • **5. SUBMISSION OF CONTRIBUTIONS.** Unless You explicitly state otherwise, any Contribution intentionally submitted for inclusion in the Work by You to the Licensor shall be under the terms and conditions of this License, without any additional terms or conditions. Notwithstanding the above, nothing herein shall supersede or modify the terms of any separate license agreement you may have executed with Licensor regarding such Contributions. • **6. TRADEMARKS.** This License does not grant permission to use the trade names, trademarks, service marks, or product names of the Licensor, except as required for reasonable and customary use in describing the origin of the Work and reproducing the content of the NOTICE file. • **7. DISCLAIMER OF WARRANTY.** Unless required by applicable law or agreed to in writing, Licensor provides the Work (and each Contributor provides its Contributions) on an "AS IS" BASIS, WITHOUT WARRANTIES OR CONDITIONS OF ANY KIND, either express or implied, including, without limitation, any warranties or conditions of TITLE, NON-INFRINGEMENT, MERCHANTABILITY, or FITNESS FOR A PARTICULAR PURPOSE. You are solely responsible for determining the appropriateness of using or redistributing the Work and assume any risks associated with Your exercise of permissions under this License. • **8. LIMITATION OF LIABILITY.** In no event and under no legal theory, whether in tort (including negligence), contract, or otherwise, unless required by applicable law (such as deliberate and grossly negligent acts) or agreed to in writing, shall any Contributor be liable to You for damages, including any direct, indirect, special, incidental, or consequential damages of any character arising as a result of this License or out of the use or inability to use the Work (including but not limited to damages for loss of goodwill, work stoppage, computer failure or malfunction, or any and all other commercial damages or losses), even if such Contributor has been advised of the possibility of such damages. • **9. ACCEPTING WARRANTY OR ADDITIONAL LIABILITY.** While redistributing the Work or Derivative Works thereof, You may choose to offer, and charge a fee for, acceptance of support, warranty, indemnity, or other liability obligations and/or rights consistent with this License. However, in accepting such obligations, You may act only on Your own behalf and on Your sole responsibility, not on behalf of any other Contributor, and only if You agree to indemnify, defend, and hold each Contributor harmless for any liability incurred by, or claims asserted against, such Contributor by reason of your accepting any such warranty or additional liability. • **END OF TERMS AND CONDITIONS**

Made in the USA
Columbia, SC
08 March 2021